MAX
notes

D1435583

William Shakespeare's

Julius Caesar

Text by
Joseph E. Scalia
(M.A., Brooklyn College)
Department of English
Hicksville High School
Hicksville, New York

Illustrations by
Thomas E. Cantillon

Research & Education Association

MAXnotes™ for
JULIUS CAESAR

Printed in the United States of America

Library of Congress Catalog Card Number 94-65956

International Standard Book Number 0-87891-948-1

MAXnotes™ is a trademark of
Research & Education Association, Piscataway, New Jersey 08854

What **MAXnotes**™ *Will Do for You*

This book is intended to help you absorb the essential contents and features of William Shakespeare's *Julius Caesar* and to help you gain a thorough understanding of the work. The book has been designed to do this more quickly and effectively than any other study guide.

For best results, this **MAXnotes** book should be used as a companion to the actual work, not instead of it. The interaction between the two will greatly benefit you.

To help you in your studies, this book presents the most up-to-date interpretations of every section of the actual work, followed by questions and fully explained answers that will enable you to analyze the material critically. The questions also will help you to test your understanding of the work and will prepare you for discussions and exams.

Meaningful illustrations are included to further enhance your understanding and enjoyment of the literary work. The illustrations are designed to place you into the mood and spirit of the work's settings.

The **MAXnotes** also include summaries, character lists, explanations of plot, and chapter-by-chapter analyses. A biography of the author and discussion of the work's historical context will help you put this literary piece into the proper perspective of what is taking place.

The use of this study guide will save you the hours of preparation time that would ordinarily be required to arrive at a complete grasp of this work of literature. You will be well-prepared for classroom discussions, homework, and exams. The guidelines that are included for writing papers and reports on various topics will prepare you for any added work which may be assigned.

The **MAXnotes** will take your grades "to the max."

Dr. Max Fogiel
Program Director

Contents

> **Each scene includes List of Characters,
> Summary, Analysis, Study Questions and
> Answers, and Suggested Essay Topics.**

SECTION ONE

Introduction

The Life and Work of William Shakespeare

William Shakespeare (1564–1616) is perhaps the most widely read English poet and dramatist in the world. His plays and poems have been translated into every major language, and his popularity, nearly 400 years after his death, is greater now than it was in his own lifetime. Yet very little is known about his personal and professional life.

He was born in Stratford-on-Avon, a rural town in Warwickshire, England. The exact date of his birth is unknown, but he was baptized in Holy Trinity Church on April 26, 1564, and was probably born on April 23. His father, John Shakespeare, was a leather tanner, glover, alderman, and bailiff in the town. His mother, Mary, was the daughter of Robert Arden, a well-to-do gentleman farmer.

It is assumed that young William attended the Stratford Grammar School, one of the best in rural England, where he received a sound classical training. When he was 13, his father's fortunes took a turn for the worse, and it is likely that Shakespeare was apprenticed to some local trade as a butcher, killing calves. He may even have taught school for a time before he married Anne Hathaway, a woman eight years older than he, in 1582. Shakespeare was 18 years old at the time. Their oldest child, Susanna, was born and baptized six months later in May 1583. One year and nine months later, twins, Hamnet and Judith, were christened in the same church. They were named for Shakespeare's friends, Hamnet and Judith Sadler.

Little more is known about these early years, but in 1587 or 1588, he left Stratford and arrived in London to become an actor and a writer. By 1592, at the age of 28, he began to emerge as a playwright. He evoked criticism in a book published by playwright Robert Greene, who referred to Shakespeare as an "upstart crow" who is "in his own conceit the only Shake-scene in the country."

Shakespeare's first published work, the long poem *Venus and Adonis*, appeared in 1593. Its success was followed by another poem, *The Rape of Lucrece*, in 1594. These narrative poems were written in the years when the London theaters were closed because of the plague, a highly contagious disease that had devastated most of Europe.

In 1594, when the theaters reopened, records indicate that Shakespeare had become a leading member of the Lord Chamberlain's Men, a company of actors for which he wrote for the rest of his 20-year career.

It was in the 1590s that Shakespeare wrote his plays on English history, several comedies, and the tragedies *Titus Andronicus* and *Romeo and Juliet*. In 1599, the year he wrote *Julius Caesar*, Shakespeare's company built a theater across the Thames River from London—the Globe. Between 1600 and 1606, Shakespeare completed his major tragedies, *Hamlet, Othello, King Lear*, and *Macbeth*. His plays were performed at court for Queen Elizabeth I, and after her death in 1603, for King James I.

He wrote very little after 1612, the year that he completed *King Henry VIII*. It was during a performance of this play in 1613 that the Globe caught fire and burned to the ground. Sometime between 1610 and 1613, Shakespeare returned to Stratford, where he owned a large house and property, to spend his remaining years with his wife, two daughters and their husbands. Shakespeare's son, Hamnet, had died in 1596.

In March of 1616, Shakespeare revised his will, leaving his daughter Susanna the bulk of his estate, and his wife "the second best bed and the furniture." A month after his will was signed, on April 23, 1616, Shakespeare died—ironically, on his birthday, like Cassius in *Julius Caesar*. He was buried in the floor near the altar of Holy Trinity Church on April 25.

The wry inscription on his tombstone reads:

> Good Friend, for Jesus' sake, forbear
> To dig the dust enclosed here;
> Blest be the man that spares these stones
> And curst be he that moves my bones.

Historical Background

In 1599, when *Julius Caesar* was first performed, Queen Elizabeth I, the Tudor Queen, was in the final years of her 45-year reign (1558–1603). It was a period of history called the "Age of Discovery," a time of scientific growth, a rebirth of the arts, and exploration of the recently discovered continents of North and South America. Historical plays were popular during Shakespeare's lifetime and people were eager to learn about worlds other than their own. A play like *Julius Caesar* taught them about Roman history, and at the same time, provided them with a mirror of their own society—a peacetime monarchy after a hundred years of warfare and before the Civil War that began in 1642.

Elizabeth's reign was one of the most secure known by the English in hundreds of years. But her throne came under attack from Roman Catholic plots to replace the Protestant monarch with a Catholic. While Shakespeare was writing *Julius Caesar*, Elizabeth's own favorite, the Earl of Essex rebelled in 1601, intending to replace the Queen's Secretary of State, Sir Robert Cecil, with a group of young aristocrats. His plan failed. But even more damaging attacks on the idea of monarchy came from loyal Puritans. Radicals like Peter Wentworth and John Field wanted democracy and called for "liberty, freedom and enfranchisement," words echoed in Shakespeare's play.

Like Julius Caesar, Queen Elizabeth had no heirs to follow her on the throne. In 1599, when she was ill, people feared that civil war and religious struggle would be the only way the question of her succession could be answered.

Although Shakespeare was writing about Rome, he was also posing questions about his own times. Who is fit to have authority? Who is fit to take this authority away? Is authority justified by legal or divine right? Can rebellion against authority ever be justified? All of these concerns can be found in *Julius Caesar.*

Performance of the Play

In September of 1599, a Swiss doctor visiting London wrote in his journal that he crossed the Thames and "there in the thatched roof witnessed an excellent performance of the tragedy of the first emperor Julius." This entry is one of the few surviving pieces of information about the production in the original Globe Theater.

We know that a performance of *Julius Caesar* included realistic sound effects for thunder and battle scenes. The actor playing Caesar probably had a pig's bladder filled with blood under his costume, and when he was stabbed, he and the conspirators were covered with blood. About 15 men played all the parts in the play, memorizing several parts each. The two female roles were played by boy apprentices. There were no woman actors in the theater at this time.

Today critics are divided over *Julius Caesar*. Some consider it flawed because it is the only Shakespearean tragedy where the title character is killed halfway through the play. Also, the focus of the action is never clear. Who is the hero of the play? Is it Caesar or Brutus? What is the message Shakespeare intends? Certainly, they agree, the play is not as powerful as *Hamlet* or *King Lear*.

In reading the play today, we tend to judge it by our modern standards and concepts of democracy and freedom. When you read the play, try to see it through the eyes of one who lived in England at the beginning of the 17th Century. It was a time of change and discovery, yet it was a time of divine right, monarchy, order and obligation. Without these things the world would be in chaos. What destroys the harmony in Caesar's Rome—Caesar's ambition for power? Cassius' jealousy? Brutus' naivete? Or the fickleness of its citizens?

Master List of Characters

Julius Caesar—*Dictator of Rome*

Marcus Antonius (Mark Antony)—*Friend of Caesar and one of the leaders of Rome after Caesar's death*

Marcus Brutus—*Friend of Caesar who kills him "for the good of Rome"*

Cassius—*Leader of the conspiracy against Caesar and brother-in-law of Brutus*

Casca—*The first conspirator to stab Caesar*

Trebonius—*Member of the conspiracy against Caesar*

Caius Ligarius—*Final member of the conspiracy, a sick man who joins them when Brutus asks him to help make Rome well*

Decius Brutus—*Conspirator who uses flattery to get Caesar to the Senate House*

Metellus Cimber—*Conspirator and brother of Publius Cimber who was banished from Rome*

Cinna—*Conspirator who urges Cassius to bring Brutus into the conspiracy to gain favorable public opinion*

Flavius and Marullus—*Tribunes who guard the rights of Roman citizens*

Octavius Caesar—*Nephew of Julius Caesar and first Roman Emperor*

Lepidus—*Ally of Antony and Octavius and one of the three rulers of Rome after Caesar's assassination*

Cicero—*Roman senator and orator later killed by Antony, Octavius, and Lepidus*

Publius—*Elderly senator and witness to Caesar's death*

Popilius Lena—*Senator who was opposed to Caesar*

Calphurnia—*Wife of Caesar who tried to keep her husband home on the day of his assassination*

Portia—*Wife of Brutus, daughter of Cato and sister of Young Cato*

Lucilius—*Officer in Brutus' army who is captured by Antony*

Titinius—*Officer in Cassius' army who commits suicide after Cassius' death*

Messala—*Officer in Brutus' army who gives Brutus information from Rome, including news of Portia's suicide*

Young Cato—*Brother-in-law of Brutus who dies in battle*

Varro and Claudius—*Soldiers under Brutus' command who wait in his tent in Sardis before the battle at Philippi*

Volumnius, Clitus, and Dardanus—*Soldiers under Brutus' command who refuse to help him commit suicide after the battle of Philippi*

Strato—*Loyal friend of Brutus who assists him in his suicide*

Lucius—*Servant of Brutus*

Pindarus—*Servant of Cassius who helps his master commit suicide*

Artemidorus—*Friend of Caesar who writes a letter warning him of the plot*

Soothsayer—*Seer into the future who tries to warn Caesar about the plot to kill him*

Cinna the Poet—*Poet on his way to Caesar's funeral who is killed by an angry mob out for revenge*

Another Poet—*Jester who enters Brutus' tent while Brutus and Cassius are arguing*

Labeo and Flavius—*Soldiers in Brutus' army*

Summary of the Play

The play begins in Rome in 44 B.C. on the Feast of Lupercal, in honor of the god Pan. Caesar has become the most powerful man in the Roman Republic and is eager to become king. Caesar, however, has many enemies who are planning his assassination. When Caesar and his entourage appear, a soothsayer warns him to "Beware the ides of March," (March 15), but Caesar is unconcerned.

Cassius tries to convince Brutus that Caesar is too ambitious and must be assassinated for the welfare of Rome. Cassius is determined to win Brutus to his cause by forging letters from citizens and leaving them where Brutus will find them. The letters attack Caesar's ambition and convince Brutus that killing Caesar is for the good of Rome.

For a month, Brutus struggles with the problem and on the morning of the ides of March, he agrees to join the others. The conspirators escort Caesar to the Senate and stab him to death.

Brutus addresses the agitated crowd and tells them why Caesar had to be killed. Then Mark Antony delivers his funeral oration and stirs the crowd to mutiny against Brutus, Cassius, and the others. The mob runs through the streets looking to avenge Caesar's death. A civil war breaks out.

Brutus and Cassius escape to Greece where they raise an army and prepare to fight Octavius and Antony in a decisive battle.

When Cassius believes he has lost the war, he convinces his servant, Pindarus, to stab him. After Brutus is defeated in a second battle, he commits suicide by running on his own sword rather than being taken prisoner back to Rome.

The play ends with the restoration of order, as Octavius and Antony become the two most powerful men in Rome.

Estimated Reading Time

The play should take the reader about five hours to complete. Since it is a five-act play, you should allocate about an hour for each act, although the time may vary depending on the number of scenes in each act. The final two acts of the play read more quickly and they may be covered in less than an hour.

(Note: All line number references in his book are based on the 1992 New Folger Library edition. If you are using a different edition, the line number references may differ slightly.)

Act I

Act 1, Scene 1

New Characters:

Flavius and Marullus: *tribunes opposed to Caesar's growing power*

Roman Citizens: *among them a cobbler and carpenter, supporters of Caesar*

Summary

The setting is February 15, 44 B.C., the Feast of Lupercal, on a street in Rome. After the death of Pompey, Caesar has returned to Rome as the most powerful man in the Republic. The play begins on a Roman street with a confrontation between Flavius and Marullus (Roman tribunes) and a crowd of citizens out to celebrate Caesar's arrival for the games. The tribunes are concerned about Caesar's growing power and popular support and how it may destroy the Roman Republic. They scold the citizens and remind them of the love and support Rome once gave Pompey, who was killed in the civil war with Caesar. Flavius and Marullus drive the crowd from the streets. They decide to pull down any banners and decorations honoring Caesar, and scatter the crowds wherever they find them in an attempt to weaken popular support for Caesar.

Analysis

The opening scene is expository. It establishes the time and

place and gives the audience an indication of what happened before the play began. It shows the political climate in Rome and the conflict surrounding Caesar. Rome, once ruled by three men (a *triumvirate*) is now in the hands of only one, Caesar, whose ambitions include becoming king. The citizens, once loyal to Pompey, one of the triumvirate, now form the base of Caesar's power. Others, represented by Flavius and Marullus, are opposed to Caesar and the threat he represents to the Roman Republic.

Flavius and Marullus drive the crowd from the streets. This

shows how easily the crowd can be manipulated and controlled. Flavius and Marullus are concerned about the welfare of the Roman state and the negative impact that Caesar's lust for power will have on its citizens. Yet the crowd seems unconcerned about politics. They are only interested in having a holiday from work, and it does not seem to matter if the celebration is for Pompey or for Caesar.

This fickleness of the commoners will surface several times throughout the play. Ultimately the commoners are used as a force to affect the politics of Rome. This will become a significant factor later in the play.

Also significant are the issues of *interpretation* and *subjectivity*. Throughout the play a character's judgment is affected by another character's interpretation of events. In this scene Flavius and Marullus are able to influence the actions of the crowd by their accounts of Pompey and how good he was for Rome. This may or may not have been true, but their perception prevails in the scene. Look for other indications of this subjective interpretation of events as Brutus considers if he should kill Caesar, the interpretation of the meaning of omens in the play, and even Pindarus' report to Cassius of the capture of Titinius in Act V.

Note Shakespeare's use of the *pun*, a play on words, in the opening lines of this scene. "I am / but , as you would say, a cobbler." (10–11) The word cobbler meant bungler as well as shoemaker. Later the character says, "all that I live by is with the / awl." (24–25) Since Shakespeare's audience was often noisy and rowdy, he opens the scene with humorous wordplay to focus his audience's attention, make them laugh, and get them to listen. Once that has been done, he returns to the essential information in the scene— the developing conflict surrounding Caesar's growing ambition.

Study Questions

1. How does Shakespeare use humor in the opening scene?

2. A pun is a play on words, two words that sound alike but have different meanings. Find two examples of puns in the opening lines of the scene.

3. How does Shakespeare show the political conflict in Rome?

4. What is the reason the cobbler tells Flavius and Marullus he is leading the people through the street?

5. What is the real reason the people are out in the street?

6. What about Pompey is revealed in this scene?

7. What information is given about Caesar?

8. How does the scene show the fickleness of the crowd?

9. Shakespeare often uses comparisons (metaphor and simile) and figurative language. What is the comparison Flavius makes in the final lines of the scene?

10. What are the intentions of Flavius and Marullus as the scene ends?

Answers

1. His characters pun, or play with word meanings. They use words that sound alike but have different meanings.

2. The word "cobbler" has two meanings, shoemaker and bungler. A "mender of bad soles" is a reference to shoemaker. This is a play on the word "souls."

   An awl is a leather punch. It is used with the word "all." Recover means to repair, as in repair shoes. Recover also means to get better as from an illness.

3. He does this by opening the play with a confrontation between the tribunes and the citizens, two opposing forces in Rome.

4. The cobbler wants them to wear out their shoes so he will get more work.

5. They are out to see Caesar and rejoice in his triumph.

6. Pompey was once loved and respected by the people of Rome.

7. Caesar was responsible for Pompey's death.

8. Flavius and Marullus are able to change the mind of the crowd with their words and convince them to disperse.

9. He compares Caesar to a bird. Driving the crowd from the street will be like plucking feathers from a bird's wing so it can not fly high.

10. They plan to go through the streets and pull down any banners that honor Caesar.

Suggested Essay Topics

1. Read through Caesar's *Commentaries*, an account of his battles in Europe and write a brief history of Caesar's rise to power.

2. Research the first triumvirate—Caesar, Crassus and Pompey. What happened to it? What were the causes and the results of the Roman Civil War?

3. The tribunes Flavius and Marullus are concerned about Caesar's rise to power. Research the role of the tribunes in Roman society and discuss their duties and responsibilities.

Act I, Scene 2

New Characters:

Caesar: *the most powerful man in the Roman Republic after the death of Pompey*

Calphurnia: *Caesar's wife*

Brutus: *friend of Caesar, concerned about the welfare of Rome*

Cassius: *brother-in-law of Brutus and leader of the conspiracy against Caesar*

Casca: *a conspirator against Caesar*

Antony: *a close friend of Caesar*

Soothsayer: *one who sees the future and tries to warn Caesar*

Summary

The setting for this scene is another Roman street on the Feast of Lupercal. Caesar enters at the head of a procession (triumph) with a flourish of trumpets, accompanied by his wife, friends, and some of the conspirators who will later stab him to death. They are on their way to the Coliseum for the traditional footrace to celebrate the Feast of Lupercal, a fertility festival in honor of the god Pan. Caesar stops the procession and calls for Calphurnia. He then orders Antony, who is dressed to run, to touch Calphurnia during the race. The Romans believed that a barren (sterile) woman touched by the winner of the race on the Feast of Lupercal would "Shake off their sterile curse." (11) As they are about to move off, a soothsayer calls to Caesar from the crowd. He warns Caesar, "Beware the ides of March." (March 15) (21) But Caesar dismisses the man as "a dreamer" and the procession continues to the Coliseum.

Cassius and Brutus remain behind. Cassius voices his concern

about Brutus' seeming coolness toward him. Brutus assures Cassius that they are still friends, explaining to Cassius that he is simply distracted. During their conversation they hear three shouts from the Coliseum, and Brutus admits he is afraid the people have chosen Caesar to be king.

Cassius then begins his campaign to undermine Caesar and his growing power. He tells Brutus that the Romans have allowed Caesar to grow too powerful and tries to show Brutus why Caesar is unfit to rule Rome. Cassius says he once saved Caesar from drowning during a swimming race, and another time he saw Caesar with a fever, crying "As a sick girl." (135) Cassius appeals to Brutus to do something before Caesar destroys the Roman Republic. Brutus says he will not live under the control of a king, and he is even ready to die for the good of Rome.

After the games end, Caesar and his entourage return. When he sees Cassius and Brutus together he recognizes the potential threat that Cassius represents. He tells Antony, "Yond Cassius has a lean and hungry look. / He thinks too much. Such men are dangerous." (204–205) He says that Cassius is never at "heart's ease" when he is in the company of someone who is better than he (Caesar). But Caesar quickly dismisses the threat posed by Cassius "for always I am Caesar." (222)

Casca, cynical and sarcastic, describes to Brutus and Cassius what happened at the Coliseum. The crowd cheered when Antony presented Caesar with a crown three times, which Caesar refused each time. According to Casca's account, the people cheered so much that their bad breath knocked Caesar down and he passed out. Brutus, however, says that Caesar has epilepsy.

Before he fell, Casca says, Caesar told the crowd that they could cut his throat if he displeased them, and Casca says he would have done it if he had a knife. When he recovered from his seizure, Caesar apologized for his words and actions, winning the forgiveness and sympathies of the crowd. Casca also tells Cassius and Brutus that Flavius and Marullus "for pulling scarves off Caesar's images, are put to silence." (296–7) This might mean they were put out of office, imprisoned, or even put to death.

Cassius recognizes Casca as another potential ally against Caesar and invites him to supper. He tells Brutus to consider all the things they have discussed. When Cassius is alone he says in a *soliloquy* (a speech made by a character who is alone on the stage) that he will write letters in different handwriting and leave them where Brutus will find them. He hopes the letters will convince Brutus that public opinion is opposed to Caesar, and move Brutus to take action.

Analysis

This scene shows Caesar's power and the attitudes of those surrounding him. This is done through Caesar's words in the opening lines, the reactions of others to him, and what others say about him. Caesar is vain, insensitive, and conceited. He humiliates his wife by publicly calling attention to her sterility. Yet Antony jumps when Caesar gives him an order. Antony responds, "When Caesar says 'Do this,' it is performed." (13) Caesar seems to be afraid of nothing. He dismisses the soothsayer as a "dreamer." This inflated opinion of himself will resurface later in the scene and several other times in the play.

The scene reveals that Brutus is troubled by Caesar's rise to power. This concern has preoccupied him to the point that he has neglected his friends. Brutus is at war with himself.

If there is a villain in the play, it is Cassius. He is jealous of Caesar and aware that Brutus can be manipulated by what he perceives to be for the good of Rome. Cassius probes Brutus by asking if he is aware of what is happening in Rome. When Brutus reacts to the shouts from the crowd, Cassius steps up his attack on Caesar. His story about saving Caesar's life may or may not be true. Angrily he points out that Caesar has become a god and that he must bow to him.

The issue of subjective interpretation is significant in this scene. Although Brutus is already considering the potential threat Caesar poses to Rome, it is Cassius' perception of Caesar that adds to Brutus' concern. Is Caesar really as great a threat as Cassius says?

When Caesar reappears, his astute political judgment is revealed when he immediately recognizes the threat that Cassius poses. He assesses Cassius as a loner who doesn't sleep, who reads, and who is generally not content with his life. Caesar knows instinctively that if any man is to be feared, it is Cassius. Yet Caesar is afraid of nothing. This pride, coupled with ambition, blinds him and makes him vulnerable. Caesar wishes to be a god, but, ironically, he suffers from certain physical afflictions. He is deaf in his left ear, and he is an epileptic.

The cynical and sarcastic Casca gives a humorous and biased account of the events that occurred at the Coliseum, revealing his own feelings toward Caesar. Caesar played to the crowd by three times refusing Antony's offer of a coronet, a small crown. Caesar may have done this because the crown offered by Antony was only symbolic, and had no power connected with it. By refusing the crown, Caesar would show the crowd that he wasn't really ambitious. According to Casca, when the crowd cheered, their bad breath knocked Caesar down. In actuality Caesar suffered an epileptic seizure. Brutus calls it "the falling sickness." Cassius makes a pun, indicating that Rome has "the falling sickness," falling down in worship before Caesar.

Casca's attitude, his account of the events and his reference to cutting Caesar's throat, indicate to that he is another candidate for the growing plot against Caesar. Cassius invites Casca to supper to recruit him into the conspiracy. Casca's news that Flavius and Marullus were silenced is another indication of Caesar's possible abuse of power.

Cassius' soliloquy is an important aspect of this scene. A soliloquy, a speech made by a character who is alone on the stage, reveals the character's true nature, thoughts, and feelings. In his soliloquy, after Casca and Brutus exit, Cassius indicates how he plans to trick Brutus into the plot against Caesar. He will forge letters indicating that Rome wants Caesar killed, and leave them where Brutus will find them. Cassius is shrewd, calculating, and ready to take advantage of Brutus for his own political and personal reasons. He knows that Brutus is well-respected in Rome, and his joining the conspiracy will give it respectability.

Study Questions

1. How is Caesar's power indicated in the scene?

2. What was the soothsayer's warning?

3. What reason does Brutus give Cassius for his coolness towards him?

4. What two stories does Brutus tell about Caesar?

5. What does Cassius compare Caesar to in lines 142–45?

6. What reasons does Caesar give Antony that Cassius is dangerous?

7. Why does Casca say Caesar fell?

8. What does Brutus mean when he says Caesar has the "falling sickness"?

9. What does Cassius mean when he says, "But you, and I / And honest Casca, we have the falling sickness"? (266–67)

10. How does Cassius plan to trick Brutus into joining the plot against Caesar?

Answers

1. When he tells Antony to touch Calphurnia in the race, Antony says, "When Caesar says 'Do this,' it is performed."

2. The Soothsayer warns, "Beware of the ides of March."

3. Brutus says that he has some private matters on his mind that are troubling him.

4. Caesar challenged Cassius to a swimming race, and Cassius had to save his life. He also saw Caesar with the fever in Spain, crying like "a sick girl."

5. He compares Caesar to a giant statue, under whose legs Romans must walk.

6. He is too thin. He is lean and hungry for power. He doesn't sleep. He reads. He is an observer. He doesn't smile or go to plays or listen to music. He thinks too much.

7. Casca says that the bad breath of the crowd knocked Caesar down.

8. Caesar suffers from epilepsy.

9. Cassius means that Romans are falling down before Caesar's power.

10. Cassius plans to forge letters and leave them where Brutus will find them. The letters will convince Brutus that public sentiment is against Caesar.

Suggested Essay Topics

1. Read Plutarch's *The Life of Caesar* and compare his account of the historical events with the events as they are depicted in Shakespeare's play.

2. History has been touched by political assassinations from Abraham Lincoln to Martin Luther King, Jr. Very often the profile of the assassin is that of a loner, a misfit, who has no friends and does not conform to the norms of society. Choose one political assassination and research the life and personality of the person responsible. Compare him to the picture Shakespeare presents of Cassius in the play.

Act I, Scene 3

New Characters:

Cicero: *a Roman senator and orator*

Cinna: *a conspirator against Caesar*

Summary

It is the night before the ides of March, and a terrible storm is raging. A frightened Casca, with his sword drawn, meets Cicero on a Roman street. Casca describes to Cicero all the unusual things he has witnessed: heaven "dropping fire," a man with his hand ablaze but not burning, a lion in the Capitol, an owl hooting in the marketplace at noon, and men on fire walking through the streets. Casca interprets all these signs to mean either the gods are engaged in civil war, or they are determined to destroy Rome. They mention Caesar's plans to be at the Capitol in the morning, and Cicero exits as Cassius enters.

Cassius is unconcerned about the storm and tells Casca that he has been daring the lightning to strike him. When Casca says all these terrible things are signs from the gods, Cassius interprets them as warnings against Caesar. Casca reveals that the senators plan to make Caesar king, and give him a crown that he may wear "every place save here in Italy." (91) Cassius says he would rather kill himself than see Caesar made king. He tells Casca of a plot to kill Caesar, and convinces him to join the conspiracy.

Cinna, another conspirator, enters and reports to Cassius that the others are waiting for him at Pompey's Porch, the covered entrance to the theater built by Pompey. Cassius gives Cinna some letters and instructs him to leave them where Brutus will find them. When Cinna leaves, Cassius tells Casca that Brutus is almost convinced to join them, and that one final push "yields him ours." (161) Casca rightly states that Brutus is well-respected in Rome, and his joining the conspiracy will give it respectability. Act I ends with them heading for Brutus' house to "wake him and be sure of him." (169)

Analysis

A month has passed, and there is a storm raging, symbolizing the political storm unfolding in Rome. Caesar, the head of state, is on the brink of assassination, and the natural order in Roman society is being threatened. Casca, like many Romans, is superstitious. He interprets these unusual events as evil omens. The gods, he thinks, are bent on destroying Rome.

Cassius sees Caesar's unbridled power as a greater evil and the surest way to destroying the Roman Republic. In his meeting with Casca, he reveals himself to be unafraid and undisturbed by events. Cassius is confident, openly daring the lightning to strike him. His mood is almost joyful as he and the other conspirators plan to rid Rome of a tyrant. Cassius calls the evening "A very pleasing night to honest men," (46) indicating that he regards his plans to kill Caesar as just and necessary. Cassius uses a similar approach to discover Casca's feelings toward Caesar and recruit him into his plot as he did with Brutus. He tells Casca that Romans have grown weak and "womanish" as Caesar has grown strong. His words are convincing and Casca, with a handshake, joins Cassius and the others against Caesar.

When Cinna arrives, Cassius identifies the other conspirators by name. Decius Brutus (not to be confused with Marcus Brutus), Trebonius, and Metellus Cimber are among them. The letters Cassius gives to Cinna are those he mentioned in his soliloquy. In the course of the month that has passed, many letters have been posted where Brutus would find them. They have had the desired effect of convincing Brutus of a public sentiment against Caesar. Cassius says of Brutus, "Three parts of him / Is ours already, and the man entire / Upon the next encounter yields him ours." (159–61) The importance of having Brutus with them is also understood by Casca who says, "O, he sits high in all the people's hearts, / And that which would appear offense in us / His countenance, like richest alchemy, / Will change to virtue and to worthiness." (162–65)

In this scene Cassius introduces the idea of suicide. He says he will kill himself before he will see Caesar made king. Elizabethan England was generally opposed to the concept of suicide, because it went against the Christian teaching that only God could take a person's life. However, the notion of suicide among Romans, as in the Japanese samurai tradition, was acceptable. Many Romans considered suicide preferable to dishonor and defeat. This will become a significant factor in Act V.

Study Questions

1. Why does Casca have his sword drawn?
2. What two "supernatural" events does Casca describe to Cicero?
3. What unusual "natural" event does he tell about?
4. Why does Casca think these unusual things are happening?
5. What information about Caesar is revealed in their conversation?
6. How is Cassius' conduct in the storm different from Casca's?
7. How does Cassius interpret all that is happening in Rome?
8. What news does Cinna bring to Cassius?
9. Why does Casca think it is important for Brutus to join with them in the plot against Caesar?
10. How does Cassius plan to put extra pressure on Brutus at the end of Act I?

Answers

1. He passed a lion walking in the streets of the Capitol.
2. A slave with his hands on fire was not burned. Men on fire were walking through the streets.
3. An owl, the bird of night, sat hooting in the marketplace at midday.
4. The gods are either at war or are trying to destroy the world.
5. He is going to the Capitol in the morning on the ides of March.
6. He is unafraid because he is an honest man. He even dares the lightning to strike him.
7. He says the gods are warning Romans against Caesar.

8. The other conspirators are assembled at Pompey's Porch and they are awaiting Cassius.

9. Public opinion of Brutus is favorable, and he will make the killing of Caesar seem like a noble act.

10. He and Casca and the others plan to go to his house and press him to join them.

Suggested Essay Topics

1. Superstition is an important part of the play and a significant factor in Roman life. Examine the superstition and the supernatural events described in this scene. Research Roman mythology and Roman superstitions. What did the Romans believe and what were they afraid of?

2. Compare the character of Casca as he is depicted in Scenes 1 and 2. How has he changed? What does the audience learn from him and why is he an important character in the play?

Act II

Act II, Scene 1

New Characters:

Lucius: *Brutus' servant*

Decius: *conspirator who plans to flatter Caesar and bring him to the Senate House*

Metellus Cimber and Trebonius: *conspirators against Caesar*

Portia: *wife of Brutus*

Caius Ligarius: *ill friend of Brutus; the last to join the conspiracy*

Summary

The setting for the scene is before three o'clock in the morning of the ides of March, and Brutus is alone in his garden. He is unable to sleep. His mind is still disturbed as he wrestles with what to do about Caesar. In a soliloquy, Brutus considers the possibilities. He has no personal feelings against Caesar, yet he must consider the good of Rome. Caesar has not yet acted irresponsibly, but once he is crowned and has power, he could change and do harm to Rome. Brutus compares Caesar to a poisonous snake. Because Caesar may be corrupted by power, Brutus decides he must be prevented from gaining power. He says, "And therefore think him as a serpent's egg, / Which, hatched, would, as his kind, grow mischievous, / And kill him in the shell." (33–35) Lucius, Brutus' servant, brings him some letters he has found. They all urge Brutus to act against Caesar.

Cassius, Casca, Cinna, Decius, Metellus Cimber, and Trebonius arrive to put more pressure on Brutus. Brutus announces his intention to join them, taking charge. First he convinces the others that they don't need Cicero in the conspiracy, and then he convinces them that Antony should not be killed with Caesar. Brutus tells Metellus to send Caius Ligarius, who has a grudge against Caesar, to see him so that Brutus may bring him into the plot. Decius says that he will use flattery to get Caesar out of his house if he decides to remain home. They leave with plans to arrive at Caesar's house at eight o'clock to escort him to the Capitol.

After they are gone, Portia, Brutus' wife, appears and begs him to confide in her what is going on. She convinces him that although she is a woman, she is strong and capable of keeping his secrets. But just as Brutus is about to tell Portia everything, an ill Ligarius arrives. Because he has such regard for Brutus, Ligarius agrees to "discard [his] sickness" (347) and follow Brutus. Brutus leads Ligarius towards Caesar's house, revealing the details of their plans as they go.

Analysis

For a month Brutus has been wrestling with his thoughts, unable to eat or sleep. Lucius, in contrast, has no difficulty falling asleep. In Shakespeare's world, sleep is reserved only for the innocent, those with untroubled minds.

While pacing in his garden Brutus decides that Caesar must be killed, not for what Caesar *is*, but for what he *may* become. His decision to kill Caesar has nothing to do with a desire for personal gain or power. Brutus is driven purely by concern for the good of Rome. He regards Caesar, his friend, as a potential threat to the well-being of the Republic. He compares Caesar to a poisonous snake that is dangerous only after it is hatched. To prevent danger, it must be killed in the shell. So Caesar must be killed before he abuses his power. The letters presented by Lucius, left by Cinna at the direction of Cassius, only reaffirm what Brutus has already decided.

When the other conspirators arrive, Brutus joins them with a handshake and commits himself to their plan to kill Caesar. Immediately he becomes their new leader, replacing Cassius. Ironically, the man who does not want power takes over, making decisions for these men throughout the rest of the play. He convinces them that they need not swear an oath to their cause, because what they are about to do is noble and important enough to bind them together.

When Metellus and the others want Cicero in the conspiracy to "purchase us a good opinion / And buy men's voices to commend our deeds," (157–58) Brutus persuades them that Cicero is unnecessary, "For he will never follow anything / That other men begin." (163–64)

When the question of killing Antony is brought up by the practical Cassius, Brutus again prevails. He says that they are "sacrificers, but not butchers," (179) and convinces them that if they kill Antony, their "course will seem too bloody." (175) It would be like cutting off Caesar's head and afterwards hacking off his arms and legs.

Cassius' desire to kill Antony, however, is based on sound political considerations. Antony, a friend of Caesar, might later cause trouble for the conspirators. Cassius rightly concludes that Antony should be killed with Caesar. The idealistic Brutus is moved by what he perceives to be right, and to him killing Antony would be wrong. His speech in lines 175–196 convinces them to let Antony live. This error, and other errors in judgment made by Brutus in Act III, will later prove disastrous.

The matter of Caesar's superstition arises when Cassius questions whether Caesar will even leave his house while so many strange phenomena are occurring. Decius says he will take advantage of Caesar's vulnerability to flattery to persuade Caesar to come to the Capitol.

As the conspirators leave, determined to meet at Caesar's house by eight o'clock, Portia enters. She begs Brutus to share his problems with her as his true wife. She kneels, telling him that even though she is a woman, she is strong enough to keep his secrets. To prove this she even gives herself a voluntary wound in the thigh without crying out. Brutus is so moved by Portia's display that he says he is not worthy of such a wife. The only thing that prevents him from telling her everything is the arrival of Caius Ligarius. In a very brief exchange with Ligarius, the esteem in which Brutus is held by his peers is revealed. The ill Ligarius ignores his own sickness because Brutus needs him for some undisclosed enterprise. It is a testimonial to the high opinion Ligarius and Rome have of Brutus.

Note Shakespeare's use of *anachronisms* (an object or event from the wrong time period) in this scene. Shakespeare was not concerned about the historical accuracy of certain details, and he mixed events from his era with those from Roman times. Sometimes these anachronisms were convenient methods to move the play along. How would the conspirators account for the time if the clock didn't strike three? (Clocks did not exist in Caesar's time.) Lucius tells Brutus that he does not recognize the men at the gate because they are wearing hats and cloaks. Neither hats nor cloaks were part of the Roman dress, but were in the 1600s. In addition, kerchiefs were worn by sick men and women in Shakespeare's England. Look for other anachronisms in the course of the play.

Study Questions

1. What reason does Brutus give in his soliloquy for killing Caesar?

2. What do the letters addressed to Brutus say?

3. Why can't Lucius identify the men with Cassius?

4. Why does Brutus oppose the idea of swearing an oath?

5. Why does Brutus object to Cicero joining the conspiracy?

6. Why does Brutus oppose killing Mark Antony?

7. How does Decius plan to get Caesar to the Capitol?

8. What advice does Brutus give the conspirators as they leave his house?

9. Why does Portia think she is strong enough to share in Brutus' plans?

10. How does Caius Ligarius prove his high regard for Brutus?

Answers

1. Brutus justifies killing Caesar for the good of Rome, fearing that he may abuse his power.

2. The letters urge him to "speak, strike and redress," to act against Caesar.

3. The men have their hats pulled down and their cloaks pulled up so their faces are hidden.

4. Brutus feels their cause is good enough to bind them to-

gether, and if it is not, they might as well go home and wait for death to take them.

5. He says Cicero will never follow what someone else began.

6. Their cause would seem too bloody, and they would be considered murderers. He thinks Antony is not dangerous.

7. He says he will use flattery.

8. He tells them to look fresh and hide their plans by smiling so their appearances won't give them away.

9. Portia is the daughter of Cato and the wife of Brutus, and she gave herself a voluntary wound in the thigh without crying out.

10. Ligarius agrees to do whatever Brutus needs him to do without knowing what it may be, even though he is sick.

Suggested Essay Topics

1. Read Plutarch's *Life of Brutus* and compare the historical account of Brutus to the character in Shakespeare's play.

2. A "tragic flaw" is a weakness of personality in a character that makes the character vulnerable, and leads to his destruction. What were Caesar's and Brutus' "tragic flaws" and how do these flaws make them vulnerable?

Act II, Scene 2

Summary

It is almost eight o'clock in the morning on the ides of March at Caesar's house. Caesar is awakened by Calphurnia crying out in her sleep. Caesar orders his servant to have the priests sacrifice an animal and bring back word of the results. Calphurnia asks her husband to stay at home because she is afraid he will be murdered, but the proud and haughty Caesar refuses to take her warning. Caesar's servant returns with word from the augurers (priests), who want Caesar to remain inside because, "They could not find a heart within the beast." (43)

Caesar interprets this differently. He says, "The gods do this in shame of cowardice. / Caesar should be a beast without a heart / If he should stay at home today for fear." (44–46) It is only when Calphurnia kneels and begs him to stay home for her sake that Caesar agrees.

As planned, Decius arrives to escort Caesar to the Senate. Caesar tells him to take word to the senators that he intends to remain home. When Decius presses him for a reason, Caesar tells him of Calphurnia's dream, where she saw a statue of Caesar oozing blood in a hundred places, with many Romans bathing their hands in it. However, Decius interprets the dream in a favorable way. He says that Caesar is the lifeblood of Rome, and the men bathing in his blood are gaining strength from him. Decius also appeals to Caesar's pride. He tells him that the senators might think Caesar is afraid if he does not show up because Calphurnia had bad dreams. Decius' appeal changes Caesar's mind. He decides to ignore his wife's fears and go to the Senate. Brutus, Cassius, and the others arrive in time to put more pressure on Caesar. The scene ends with them leaving together for the Senate House.

Analysis

This scene parallels the preceding scene, where Portia influences Brutus, only to be interrupted by Ligarius. Here Calphurnia convinces Caesar to stay at home, only to have Decius interrupt, changing Caesar's mind.

Superstition and supernatural forces again play an important part in this scene. In an attempt to convince her husband to stay home, Calphurnia describes fantastic events she has witnessed or heard about, and interprets them as omens meant to warn Caesar. She tells of graves yielding up their dead, a lioness giving birth in the streets of the city, and blood dripping from the clouds onto the Capitol, events similar to those extraordinary occurrences mentioned earlier by Casca. Calphurnia pleads with Caesar to give into her fears. "Caesar, I never stood on ceremonies, / But now they fright me." (13–14) But because of his pride, Caesar is unmoved. He says, "Cowards die many times before their deaths; / The valiant never taste of death but once." (34–35) When his servant brings word that the augurers could not find a heart in the beast they sacrificed, Caesar interprets it to mean the gods would consider him a coward without a heart if he does not go to the Senate. It is only when Calphurnia kneels to him, as Portia did with Brutus, that he consents. For an instant a tender and human side of Caesar is revealed. But when Calphurnia tells Caesar to say he is sick, it is too much for his pride to lie to "greybeards." When he does agree to send Decius to the Senate with his decision, Caesar says, "Tell them that I will not come today. / Cannot is false, and that I dare not falser. / I will not come today." (66–68) It must be made clear to the senators that Caesar is in control.

After hearing Calphurnia's dream, Decius interprets it in a favorable way. He says it is a good omen, that Caesar is the center of Rome and from him "great Rome shall suck / Reviving blood." (92–93) He convinces Caesar to go by telling him that the Senate plans to give him a crown, and they may change their mind if Caesar does not come. There are those who will laugh at Caesar and think him a coward if he hides himself at home because Calphurnia had bad dreams. This is too much for Caesar to bear, and he changes his mind once again and agrees to go to the Senate. The man who says he hates flatterers is flattered and lured to his death.

Study Questions

1. Why is Caesar concerned when the scene begins?

2. What is Calphurnia's request of Caesar?

3. What is Caesar's response to Calphurnia's concern he might be killed?

4. What was the result of the sacrifice performed by the augurers?

5. What reasons does Caesar give Decius for staying home?

6. What was Calphurnia's dream?

7. How does Decius use flattery to get Caesar to change his mind?

8. How does Decius interpret Calphurnia's dream?

9. What does Trebonius say when Caesar tells him to stay by?

10. What is the irony in Caesar's last lines in the scene?

Answers

1. A storm is raging and Calphurnia had a dream that Caesar was murdered.

2. She wants him to stay at home. Calphurnia is afraid for his safety because of the unusual events that are going on and because of her dream.

3. Caesar's response is, "Cowards die many times before their deaths; / The valiant never taste of death but once."

4. The augurers could not find a heart in the beast they sacrificed and they want Caesar to stay at home.

5. Caesar tells Decius that he is staying home because Calphurnia wants him to.

6. Calphurnia dreamed a statue of Caesar was spouting blood and Romans were washing their hands in it.

7. Decius interprets Calphurnia's dream in a favorable way. He tells Caesar that people will think Caesar is a coward if he doesn't go to the Senate House. He says the senate may change their minds about giving Caesar a crown.

8. Caesar is the lifeblood of Rome, and Romans, bathing in his blood, derive strength from him.

9. He says, in an aside, that he will stay so close that Caesar's friends will wish Trebonius had been further away.

10. He regards the conspirators as friends, having no idea they plan to kill him within the hour.

Suggested Essay Topics

1. Compare Caesar in Act I, Scene 2 to the Caesar that appears in this scene. How is he the same? How is he different? What does he fear and what are the forces that influence him?

2. Wives play a key role in Act II, Scenes 1 and 2. How do the wives of Brutus and Caesar try to influence their husbands? Are they successful?

Act II, Scenes 3 and 4

New Character:

Artemidorus: *teacher and friend of some of the conspirators; he has learned about the plot against Caesar*

Summary

The setting is a Roman street on the ides of March shortly before the planned assassination. Artemidorus, a teacher and friend of some of the conspirators, has learned about the plot to kill Caesar. He has written a letter naming each man and warning Caesar to be on his guard. He plans to wait for Caesar to pass and then present the letter as a suitor looking for a political favor.

At the same time, on another part of the street, an agitated Portia tells Lucius to run to the Capitol and report back to her everything his master, Brutus, says and does. The confused boy is unsure of what the distracted Portia wants him to do and he hesitates. When Portia sees the soothsayer passing by his way to the Capitol, she asks him if he knows about any harm intended toward Caesar. The soothsayer responds, "None that I know will be, much that I fear may chance." (Sc. 4, 38) He tells her that he plans to speak to Caesar when he passes.

In an aside, Portia wishes Brutus success in his enterprise and she sends Lucius off on his errand.

Analysis

How Artemidorus learned about the plot is not explained, but his information is correct and up-to-date. His list of conspirators includes Ligarius, who joined Brutus only recently. His letter cautions Caesar against overconfidence. "If thou beest not immortal, look about you. Security gives way to conspiracy." (Sc. 3, 6–7) It is precisely Caesar's sense of his own immortality, his attitude that he *is* a god, that makes him so vulnerable.

Portia's behavior in Scene 4 indicates that she knows what is about to occur. Because Shakespeare does not say exactly how she knows, we must assume she has either been told by Brutus, or has figured it out for herself. The issue of her being a "weak" woman, brought up in the previous scene, is mentioned again. "O constancy, be strong upon my side; / Set a huge mountain 'tween my heart and tongue. / I have a man's mind but a woman's might. / How hard it is for women to keep counsel!" (Sc. 4, 7–10) Portia is now so agitated she can hardly contain herself, and is about to burst. Her orders to Lucius are unclear and his response is almost humorous. "Madam, what should I do? / Run to the Capitol, and nothing else? / And so return to you, and nothing else?" (Sc. 4, 12–14). Her exchange with the soothsayer makes it clear she knows there is a plot to "harm" Caesar.

Since all of the roles in Shakespeare's plays were acted by males, Portia's comment about a man's mind and a woman's might is a joke that wouldn't have been missed by the audience in the Globe Theater.

Study Questions

1. How does Shakespeare add the element of suspense in these two short scenes?

2. What is Artemidorus' warning?

3. What does Artemidorus mean when he says, "Security gives way to conspiracy"? (Sc. 3, 7–8)

4. How does he plan to give Caesar his letter?

5. Why doesn't Lucius carry out Portia's request?

6. What does Portia mean in her aside, "O constancy, be strong upon my side; / Set a huge mountain 'tween my heart and tongue. / I have a man's mind but a woman's might. / How hard it is for women to keep counsel!" (Sc. 4, 7–10)?

7. What does she tell Lucius to do?

8. What does the soothsayer tell Portia he plans to do?

9. What is Portia's wish for Brutus?

10. How does Portia try to cover up being overheard by Lucius?

Answers

1. He provides Caesar with two possibilities of saving his life: through Artemidorus' letter or the soothsayer.

2. Artemidorus warns Caesar to be on his guard if he is not immortal.

3. He means that overconfidence on Caesar's part opens the way to conspiracy and death.

4. He will wait on the street as a suitor looking for some political favor and present the letter to Caesar when he passes.

5. Portia does not make her intentions clear.

6. She is afraid she will not be able to keep Brutus' plans a secret because she is a "weak" woman.

7. Portia tells Lucius to bring back word as to how Brutus looks, what Caesar does, and which suitors present themselves to Caesar.

8. He will go down the street and speak to Caesar when he comes by and try to warn him about the possible danger.

9. She hopes the heavens will help him in his enterprise.

10. She tells him Brutus has a suit (a request) that Caesar will not grant him.

Suggested Essay Topics

1. Rome was a republic that depended on slavery similar to the United States until the 1860s. Research the history of slavery in Rome. Where did the slaves come from? What roles did they play in the Republic? What was a slave's life like? What rights and responsibilities did they have? What were the rights and responsibilities of Roman citizens?

2. Compare the characters of Calphurnia and Portia in terms of how they are portrayed by Shakespeare in this act. How are the two women similar? Compare the two scenes involving these two wives and their husbands. What purpose do the scenes serve?

Act III

Act III, Scene 1

New Characters:

Lepidus: *one of the three rulers of Rome after Caesar's death*

Publius: *elderly Roman senator who escorts Caesar to the Senate*

Popilius Lena: *senator who wishes success to Cassius*

Servant: *messenger from Octavius*

Summary

Caesar arrives at the Senate House on the ides of March. Artemidorus tries to give Caesar his warning letter, as Decius offers Caesar a petition. Artemidorus presses Caesar to read his letter first because it "touches Caesar nearer." (7) Caesar responds, "What touches us ourself shall be last served." (8) In other words, he ignores the letter because it is of a personal nature. Cassius is afraid that their plans are known when Popilius, a senator, says to him, "I wish your enterprise today may thrive." (14)

Cassius tells Casca to act quickly. Trebonius, as prearranged, removes Antony from the scene. Under the pretext of begging repeal of a banishment decree imposed by Caesar on Publius Cimber, brother of Metellus, they surround Caesar and isolate him from the rest of the senators. As Caesar rejects each of their appeals, the conspirators tighten the circle around him. Casca is the first to strike, and, after each of the conspirators attack Caesar, Brutus is

the last to stab him. Mortally wounded, Caesar says his last words, "*Et tu, Brutĕ?*—Then fall, Caesar," (85) and dies.

Panic ensues as the senators run from the Senate House. Under the direction of Brutus, the conspirators bathe their hands and swords in Caesar's blood and prepare to go into the streets. But before they can tell the Romans what has happened, Antony's servant enters and begs for permission for his master to come and speak to all of them. Brutus agrees, but before Antony's arrival, Cassius again considers the possibility of killing Antony.

When Antony arrives he tells the conspirators that he is ready to die, if that is their plan. Brutus assures Antony that there is no harm intended toward him, or anyone else. Reassured by Brutus, Antony shakes their bloody hands and asks for permission to bring

Caesar's body to the marketplace and to speak at Caesar's funeral. Again Brutus is quick to agree, and again Cassius objects. Brutus overrides the objection and tells Antony that he may speak, but only with certain restrictions. Antony may not blame the conspirators for killing Caesar, although he may say good things about Caesar. He must say he speaks by permission from the same pulpit after Brutus speaks.

After they leave, Antony declares his true feelings in a powerful soliloquy. He predicts a violent and bloody civil war, and he vows revenge for Caesar's death. A messenger arrives with news that young Octavius, Caesar's nephew, has arrived outside of Rome. Antony tells the messenger to wait until after his funeral speech, and then return to Octavius with news as to whether or not it is safe or not for him to enter Rome. Together they carry Caesar's body to the marketplace.

Analysis

Time is running out for Caesar, but there are still two possibilities that may save his life. The first is the soothsayer and the other is Artemidorus. Caesar dismisses the soothsayer when he sees him with his mocking, "The ides of March are come." (1) Then, he ignores Artemidorus' letter because it is personal business. Ironically, this man who regards himself as a god, who identifies himself as the center of Rome, who uses the words "us ourself" when he refers to himself, cuts himself off from possible salvation by putting himself last.

Fearing detection because their security has been compromised, Cassius indicates he will kill himself rather than live under Caesar. But it becomes clear that Popilius, a senator who wishes Cassius well, does not intend to warn Caesar, and the conspirators are free to carry out their plan. Trebonius is the only conspirator who doesn't stab Caesar. His purpose is to lead Antony off and prevent him from coming to Caesar's aid.

As he begins the day's proceedings, Caesar's ego is apparent. He says, "What is now amiss / That Caesar and his Senate must redress?" (34–35) Clearly, Caesar considers Rome and the Senate to belong to him. In his exchange with the conspirators, Caesar will not reconsider his decision banishing Publius Cimber. He says he is incapable of making mistakes. "Know: Caesar doth not wrong." (52) He considers himself no "ordinary man" and he can not be swayed by flattery.

However, Caesar's assessment of himself is not very accurate. He has already made some serious mistakes by dismissing the many warnings he has received, and by thinking the people around him are his friends. Also, Decius was able to flatter Caesar into changing his mind about coming to the Senate. Nevertheless, he says to Cassius, "I could be well moved, if I were as you. / If I could pray to move, prayers would move me. / But I am constant as the Northern Star." (64–66) He says that trying to change Caesar's mind is an impossibility, like trying to lift Mount Olympus. The concern

Brutus had in his garden about Caesar seems to be justified by Caesar's inflexibility.

Casca is the first to stab Caesar. It is fitting that Brutus be the last. Caesar's words to him—*Et tu Brutè?* (and thou, Brutus?)—indicate his disbelief that his friend could do such a thing.

In the panic that follows Caesar's death, Metellus warns the conspirators to "Stand fast together." (96) But Brutus takes charge and assures the frightened senators that "Ambition's debt is paid." (91) To mark themselves as the men who killed Caesar and gave their country "Liberty, freedom and enfranchisement," (89) Brutus tells them to bathe their hands in Caesar's blood. With this act Calphurnia's dream comes true. Brutus is so blinded by delusions of his own nobility that he goes so far as to suggest that the conspirators have done Caesar a favor by killing him: " . . . Death is a benefit / So we are Caesar's friends that have abridged / his time of fearing death." (115-17)

The arrival of Antony provides another opportunity to study the differences between the idealistic Brutus and the practical Cassius. Brutus is innocent, to the point of being naive. Because he believes his motives for killing Caesar are noble and pure, and because any reasonable Roman would recognize them as such, Brutus has no problem with Antony's request to speak at Caesar's funeral. Since they all acted for the good of Rome, how could Antony, or any Roman, not understand? Cassius however, instinctively sees the political truth and knows the problems Antony may cause them. His strenuous objections are downplayed by Brutus, who thinks he can allay Cassius' fears by imposing restrictions on Antony. He tells Antony, "You shall not in your funeral speech blame us / But speak all good you can devise of Caesar / And say you do't by our permission, / . . . And you shall speak / In the same pulpit whereto I am going, / After my speech is ended." (270–76)

When the others leave, the bloody Antony, who has shaken hands with each of the conspirators, indicates his true intentions in a soliloquy. He vows revenge for Caesar's murder, and he promises to throw Italy into such a violent civil war, "That mothers shall but smile when they behold / Their infants quartered with the hands of war, / All pity choked with custom of fell deeds." (293–95)

The arrival of a messenger at the end of the scene introduces

Octavius, Caesar's young nephew, who has an important role in the rest of the play.

Study Questions

1. Why does Caesar not read Artemidorus' letter?
2. Why does Cassius think their assassination plan has been discovered?
3. Why does Caesar get angry at Metellus?
4. What does Brutus tell the frightened senators after Caesar's assassination?
5. How does Calphurnia's dream come true?
6. What does Antony want from the conspirators?
7. What restrictions does Brutus place on Antony when he allows him to speak at the funeral?
8. What does Antony predict in his soliloquy?
9. What information does the messenger bring to Antony?
10. What are Antony's intentions as the scene ends?

Answers

1. He says because it is personal business it can wait. He puts affairs of state before personal matters.
2. Popilius Lena wishes him good luck in their enterprise and then he goes and talks to Caesar.
3. He thinks Metellus is trying to flatter him into changing his mind. Caesar says he cannot be swayed.
4. He says no harm is intended toward anyone else and they shouldn't be afraid.
5. Brutus tells the conspirators to bathe their hands and swords in Caesar's blood to mark them as the men who killed Caesar and gave their country freedom.
6. First he says he wants to die by Caesar if they intend to kill him. Then when he realizes he will be allowed to live, he

wants to know why Caesar was killed and to speak at Caesar's funeral.

7. Antony may not blame the conspirators for killing Caesar, though he may say good things about Caesar. He must say he speaks by their permission. He must speak from the same place as Brutus after Brutus has first addressed the crowd.

8. He predicts a bloody civil war, with dead bodies waiting for burial, and revenge for Caesar's death.

9. Octavius, summoned by Caesar, has arrived outside of Rome.

10. He plans to stir up the crowd and then send word to Octavius if it is safe for him to enter Rome.

Suggested Essay Topics

1. A soliloquy is an important device to expose information and give the reader insight into a character. In a soliloquy, the character speaks the truth. Read Antony's soliloquy in this scene again. What truth does it reveal about Antony who has just apparently reconciled with the men who killed his friend, Caesar?

2. How does Caesar's "tragic flaw" of pride and ambition enable the events in this scene to occur? How could these events have been prevented?

Act III, Scenes 2 and 3

New Characters:

Plebeians: *Roman citizens at Caesar's funeral*

Servant: *messenger from Octavius*

Cinna the Poet: *a poet with the same name as one of the conspirators*

Summary

The setting is in the marketplace at Caesar's funeral shortly after his death. The agitated crowd demands an explanation for

Caesar's assassination. Cassius leaves with some of the crowd to
give his version of why Caesar was killed, while Brutus remains
behind with the others to give his own account of the events. Brutus
explains that although he was Caesar's friend, and loved him, Caesar was ambitious and had to be killed for the good of Rome. If
allowed to live, Caesar would have made slaves of all the Romans.
He tells the crowd that he is ready to kill himself with the same
dagger he used to kill Caesar, if they think he did wrong. But they

are so moved by his speech that the crowd wants to erect statues in Brutus' honor and make him king. Brutus declines their offer, and after telling them to listen to what Antony has to say, Brutus leaves.

Antony faces a hostile audience when he ascends into the pulpit and begins his oration with the words, "Friends, Romans, countrymen, lend me your ears." (Sc. 2, 82) Slowly he wins them over, proving that Caesar was not ambitious. He calls the conspirators "honorable men," yet he shows them to be traitors. Antony cries for Caesar and produces his will. He tells the angry citizens that he dare not read the will because it might stir them to mutiny and rage against Cassius and Brutus. He shows them Caesar's bloody cloak and his mutilated body, stirring them up with every word. And when he finally reads the will, revealing the generous legacy Caesar left the citizens of Rome, the crowd is transformed into an angry mob, out of control and intent on revenge against the conspirators. Antony is quite pleased with these results, and with the news brought by a messenger from Octavius, that Cassius and Brutus have fled Rome.

In the next scene, Cinna, the poet, on his way to Caesar's funeral, is confronted by a mob carrying torches and clubs. They demand answers to their questions, and when Cinna tells them his name they threaten to kill him as a conspirator. He says he isn't one of the conspirators, but a poet. The angry mob kills him anyway, "for his bad verses," (Sc. 3, 31) and then runs off to burn the houses of the conspirators.

Analysis

The scene provides another example of subjective interpretation, and shows how it affects the actions of others. The crowd of citizens is moved first by Brutus' picture of Caesar, and then turned into an angry mob by a totally different Caesar painted by Antony. The fickleness of the Roman people, evident from the first scene of the play, becomes more apparent now. After Caesar's assassination, the angry crowd, commoners who were the foundation of Caesar's power, demand an explanation from the bloody men who just murdered their hero. Brutus is so sure killing Caesar was the right thing to do that he is ready to die for his convictions. He is so convincing in arguing that Caesar's ambition would have destroyed the Roman Republic that the crowd is eager to "Bring him with triumph home unto his house. / Give him a statue with his ancestors. / Let him be Caesar." (Sc. 2, 51–53) In their response lies the irony. Brutus killed Caesar, who would be king, to deliver Rome from tyranny, and these same people would make their liberator king. They have missed the point behind Brutus' actions and oration.

Antony's funeral speech is the dramatic high point of the play. Not only is he able to stir up the Romans into a frenzied mob, as he predicted he would in his soliloquy in Act III, but he does so while fulfilling the restrictions imposed on him by Brutus. Antony cautiously ascends to the same pulpit as Brutus, after Brutus speaks,

and he says he speaks by permission. He doesn't blame the conspirators, but uses the phrase "honorable men" with such unmistakable irony that the crowd calls them villains and murderers. His pun, "O judgment thou has fled to brutish beasts," (Sc. 2, 106) followed by his tears, has an electrifying effect on his audience. Antony manipulates the crowd by showing them Caesar's will, and then telling them he cannot read it. He holds off their demands to read it, allowing their emotions to build. Next, Antony, who was not present when Caesar was killed, shows them Caesar's cloak, and dramatically points out where each of the conspirators stabbed. "Look, in this place ran Cassius' dagger through. / See what a rent the envious Casca made. / Through this the well-beloved Brutus stabbed." (Sc. 2, 186–8) It is a theatrical ploy, but most effective. The crowd even forgets about the will, until Antony reminds them. He reads the will: "To every Roman citizen he gives, / To every several man, seventy-five dracmas (silver coins)." (Sc. 2, 255–6) And, "Moreover, he hath left you all his walks, / His private arbors, and new-planted orchards, / On this side Tiber." (Sc. 2, 261–3) This pushes the crowd into a frenzy that Antony sets loose on Rome.

In a move of tactical brilliance, Antony announces himself as a lamb so he can later pounce like a lion:

> I come not, friends, to steal away your hearts
> I am no orator, as Brutus is;
> But (as you know me all) a plain blunt man
> That loves my friend, and that they know full well
> That gave me public leave to speak of him.
> For I have neither writ, nor words, nor worth
> Action, nor utterance, nor the power of speech
> To stir men's blood; I only speak right on. (Sc. 2, 228–235)

By creating the illusion that he will not attempt to stir the crowd, he lowers its resistance, opens its heart, and firmly sinks in his teeth. In such a way, Antony easily manipulates the crowd, by claiming he is not the manipulative type. Furthermore, Antony cleverly attributes his own powers of manipulation to the unwitting Brutus by suggesting that he is not an orator like Brutus. Antony's political cunning is obvious, especially in contrast to Brutus' sincerity (albeit misguided).

Cinna, the poet, becomes the first victim of the mob. He is in the wrong place at the wrong time, drawn there by some unknown, supernatural forces. "I dreamt tonight that I did feast with Caesar, / And things unluckily charge my fantasy. / I have no will to wander forth of doors, / Yet something leads me forth." (Sc. 3, 1–4) He is surrounded by people out for revenge, who ask him many questions but are not interested in his answers. He responds to one of these questions about being married or single, "Wisely I say, I am a bachelor." (Sc. 3, 17) They then threaten to beat him for implying "they are fools that marry." (Sc. 3, 18–19) Clearly the mob is out for blood. Ultimately they kill him just for being there, using his "bad verses" as their justification.

Act III ends with Rome in complete chaos and on the brink of civil war.

Study Questions

1. How does Brutus justify the killing of Caesar to the people of Rome?

2. What is the crowd's reaction to Brutus' speech?

3. What two reasons does Antony give to prove Caesar wasn't ambitious?

4. How does Antony use irony in his funeral speech?

5. What is the pun Antony uses in line 114 of Scene 3?

6. How does Antony use Caesar's cloak to manipulate the crowd?

7. How does Antony say that Caesar died?

8. What is the news that the messenger brings to Antony at the end of the scene?

9. Why is Cinna out on the streets?

10. What is the excuse the mob uses to kill Cinna?

Answers

1. Caesar was ambitious and Brutus says he killed him because he loved Rome more than Caesar.

2. They want to erect statues in his honor and make him king.

3. Caesar was too sensitive and cried when he saw the poor crying. "Ambition should be made of sterner stuff." (Sc. 2, 101) Also, Caesar refused the crown three times when Antony offered it to him on the feast of Lupercal.

4. He uses the words "honorable men" repeatedly, twisting the meaning so the crowd understands that he means the exact opposite.

5. He uses the phrase "brutish beasts," a pun on Brutus' name and his bestial behavior in killing Caesar.

6. He points out the rips in the cloak and describes where each of the conspirators stabbed Caesar, even though he wasn't there to witness the event.

7. He says that Caesar died of a broken heart when he was stabbed by Brutus who was Caesar's angel (best friend).

8. Octavius is outside of Rome, and Brutus and Cassius have fled the city.

9. He is on his way to Caesar's funeral, driven out of doors by some unknown force.

10. They kill him for writing bad poetry.

Suggested Essay Topics

1. Compare the funeral speeches of Brutus and Antony. What are their purposes? How effective is each speech? How does each speech reveal important aspects of both characters?

2. The fickleness of the crowd is an important issue in the play. Brutus and Antony both depend on it. How are they able to manipulate the crowd in this scene? What other devices do they use in their funeral speeches to win the support of the crowd? Which speech is more effective and why? Give reasons for your opinions.

Act IV

Act IV, Scene 1

New Characters:

Octavius: *Caesar's nephew and one of the three leaders to rule Rome after his death*

Lepidus: *the third leader to rule Rome after Caesar's death*

Summary

The setting is a house in Rome some time after Caesar's death. The Republic is in turmoil, as Antony predicted. Rome is in the hands of Antony, Octavius, and Lepidus. They are compiling a death list of their political enemies. Antony sends Lepidus to "fetch" Caesar's will so they might reduce some of the legacies mentioned by Antony to the citizens in his funeral speech. When Lepidus leaves, Antony tells Octavius that Lepidus is unfit to have so much power. Antony plans to use Lepidus to achieve his political objectives and then cut him off. They talk about Brutus and Cassius, who have fled the country and are raising an army in Greece. Antony and Octavius make plans to muster their own forces to fight them.

Analysis

Act IV addresses the corrupting effects of power. Rome is on the brink of a terrible civil war. Antony has joined forces with Octavius and Lepidus to become one of the three most powerful men in Rome. They are the second triumvirate to rule the Republic. (Caesar, Pompey, and Crassus were the first.)

    To solidify their political power, and because they have many enemies in Rome, they are making a list of Roman senators and citizens they plan to execute. Their decisions are cold and unfeeling. In a political tit-for-tat, Lepidus consents to listing his own brother, provided that Antony agrees to include his nephew. Ironically, their total disregard for life goes beyond anything Brutus feared Caesar might do. Their greed is made more evident in their plan to change Caesar's will for their personal gain.

    The moral flaw in Antony's character can also be seen when

he reveals his contempt for Lepidus. When Octavius calls Lepidus "a tried and valiant soldier," (32) Antony compares Lepidus to his horse who "must be taught and trained and bid go forth." (39) It is Antony's intention to use Lepidus as a practical means to his desired end, much as Cassius used Brutus. It is not a flattering picture of the man who rose to great heights in Act III, and who is about to lead Rome into civil war.

Study Questions

1. Why are Antony, Octavius, and Lepidus together in the scene?

2. How does Shakespeare show their callousness?

3. Why does Antony send Lepidus to Caesar's house?

4. What is Antony's true opinion of Lepidus?

5. Why did Antony pick Lepidus as one of the new leaders of Rome?

6. What does Antony compare Lepidus to?

7. What is Octavius' assessment of Lepidus?

8. What is Antony's response to Octavius?

9. What news does Antony tell Octavius about Brutus and Cassius?

10. Why does Octavius agree with Antony's plan to go after Cassius and Brutus?

Answers

1. They are making a list of people to be killed in order to tighten their control in Rome.

2. Lepidus agrees to have his brother placed on the list if Antony agrees to condemn his own nephew.

3. He sends him for Caesar's will. They plan to reduce what Caesar left to the Roman citizens.

4. He thinks Lepidus is fit to be sent on errands, but not fit to be one of the three most powerful men in the world.

5. Antony needs Lepidus to gain favorable public opinion.

6. He compares him to a mule that carries a load from one place to another and then is turned loose to graze. He also compares him to his horse.

7. Octavius says Lepidus is an experienced and brave soldier.

8. Antony says his horse is also a brave soldier, who must be taught to fight, run, and stop, and be ruled by Antony, as must Lepidus.

9. They are raising an army in Greece and preparing for war.

10. He says they are surrounded by many enemies in Rome and those who pretend to be their friends are not.

Suggested Essay Topics

1. What does this scene reveal about Octavius? What new insight does it give into Antony's character, and how does that effect your opinion of him?

2. Antony and Octavius will become the focus of attention for the remainder of the play and Shakespeare will write about them again in *Antony and Cleopatra*. Little is said or known of Lepidus. Research the life of Lepidus. What is his background? Where did he come from, and what happened to him after the civil war with Brutus and Cassius?

Act IV, Scenes 2 and 3

New Characters:

Pindarus: *servant to Cassius taken prisoner in Partheia*

Lucilius: *officer in Brutus' army*

Messala: *officer in Brutus' army*

Titinius: *friend of Cassius and Officer in his army*

Varro: *soldier in Brutus' army*

Claudius: *soldier in Brutus' army*

Poet: *jester who enters Brutus' tent*

Caesar's Ghost

Soldiers

Summary

The setting is the camp of Brutus in Sardis, Greece. Brutus and his soldiers are awaiting the arrival of Cassius and his army. When Pindarus, a slave to Cassius, brings his master's greetings, Brutus indicates his misgivings about the course of events. He confides to Lucilius, one of his officers, that he has regrets about killing Caesar.

As soon as Cassius arrives in camp he begins to quarrel with Brutus. Brutus cautions him that they should not fight in front of the troops they will soon lead into battle, so they move into Brutus' tent to continue their argument.

Cassius is angry because a friend of his, Lucius Pella, has been punished for taking bribes and Brutus ignored letters that Cassius wrote in the man's defense. Brutus attacks Cassius for defending Pella, and he attacks Cassius' own reputation for taking bribes. As their tempers flare, they come to the point of drawing swords. Cassius physically threatens Brutus, who dismisses him as a "slight man," (Sc. 3, 40) and reminds him that they killed Caesar for the sake of justice and not for personal gain.

Brutus is angry because he sent a request to Cassius for money to pay his troops and Cassius refused. Cassius denies refusing the money, and is so disturbed by what Brutus thinks that he offers him his dagger and tells Brutus to kill him. This calms Brutus and he and Cassius shake hands, reaffirming their friendship. Brutus tells Cassius he is distraught because he learned of his wife's death in letters from Rome. Depressed by Brutus' flight, she committed suicide.

Messala and Titinius, officers in their armies, enter with news from Rome, confirming Portia's death, along with the murder of 70 to 100 Roman senators.

Brutus turns their attention back to "our work alive," a battle plan to meet the advancing enemy armies. Brutus wants to march to Philippi, while Cassius thinks they should remain where they are and have their enemies come to them. Brutus argues that they are in unfriendly territory, at the peak of their strength, and they must seize the opportunity before they weaken. Once again Cassius gives in to Brutus, and the decision is made to set off for Philippi in the morning.

While reading a book in his tent Brutus begins to doze. In this twilight of consciousness, the ghost of Caesar appears to him. The ghost says he is Brutus' evil spirit, and that he will see Brutus again at Philippi. Before Brutus awakens fully the ghost is gone. Brutus calls Varro and Claudius, soldiers in his army, and tells them to send word to Cassius to move his troops to Philippi at once.

Analysis

As Scene 1 showed the corrupting effects of power on Antony, Octavius, and Lepidus, these scenes indicate the breakdown in the relationship between Brutus and Cassius. The passage of time, the unexpected chaos that has developed in Rome, the reaction of the Roman people, and Cassius' behavior have made Brutus wish "Things done undone." (Sc. 2, 9) Nothing is what he expected.

His meeting with Cassius in the camp at Sardis is a confrontation over money, but there are deeper issues addressed during their fight in the tent. Cassius is angry because he thinks Brutus wronged him when he disregarded the letters Cassius wrote in defense of Lucius Pella. Brutus, however, thinks that Cassius wronged himself to sanction bribery. He questions Cassius' honesty and accuses him of taking bribes and selling his favors to the highest bidder. Cassius is infuriated, but Brutus, whose motives are always noble,

reminds Cassius that they killed Caesar for justice, not for money.

Cassius warns Brutus not to bait him or he may do something he will be sorry for. Brutus responds, "You have done that you should be sorry for," (Sc. 3, 74) meaning the assassination of Caesar. At the point of drawing their swords, Brutus tells Cassius he is not afraid of him. "There is no terror, Cassius, in your threats, / For I am armed so strong in honesty / That they pass by me as the idle wind, / Which I respect not." (Sc. 3, 75–77) He confronts Cassius with the fact that when Brutus needed money to pay his army, Cassius refused to send it to him.

Cassius is so troubled by what Brutus says that he calls upon Antony and Octavius to come and avenge themselves on Cassius. Then Cassius offers Brutus his sword and tells him to use it on him:

> There is my dagger,
> And here my naked breast; within, a heart
> Dearer than Pluto's mine, richer than gold.
> If thou be'st a Roman, take it forth.
> I that denied thee gold will give my heart.
> Strike as thou didst at Caesar, for I know
> When thou didst hate him worst, thou lovedst him better
> Than ever thou lovedst Cassius. (Sc. 3, 111–19)

His words calm Brutus and they shake hands and make up. It is then that Brutus tells Cassius about the unusual circumstances of Portia's death. She committed suicide by swallowing burning coals.

Titinius and Messala arrive to make plans for battle. Messala confirms the deaths of Portia and 70–100 senators, including Cicero. They are the casualties of the death list compiled by Antony, Octavius, and Lepidus earlier.

The rest of the scene serves to show that Brutus is still making the decisions. Despite the objections of Cassius, Brutus convinces them it would be better to march to Philippi. The Sardians become Brutus' soldiers due to forced loyalty, and thus, may join the enemy. Brutus says it would be safer to put the Sardians at their backs and march out to meet the enemy. He uses a sea metaphor to make his point:

> There is a tide in the affairs of men
> Which taken at the flood, leads on to fortune;
> Omitted, all the voyage of their life
> Is bound in shallows and in miseries.
> On such a full sea are we now afloat,
> And we must take the current when it serves
> Or lose our ventures. (Sc. 3, 249–55)

Throughout the play Brutus has made serious errors in judgment in letting Antony live, and allowing him to speak at Caesar's funeral. It is the decision to march to Philippi however, that will prove to be a fatal mistake for Cassius and Brutus.

The scene ends with another appearance of the supernatural, a visit from Caesar's ghost, as Antony predicted earlier in his soliloquy in Act III. But is it really Caesar's spirit Brutus sees as he dozes over a book, or Brutus having qualms of conscience for what he has done? The apparition foreshadows Philippi, where Brutus will see Caesar's ghost again.

Study Questions

1. Why is Brutus concerned about Lucilius' account of his meeting with Cassius?

2. Why does Brutus tell Cassius to come into his tent?

3. Why is Cassius angry with Brutus?

4. Why is Brutus angry with Cassius?

5. Why does Brutus say he is not afraid of Cassius' threats?

6. What is the advice given to Cassius and Brutus by the poet?

7. What is the news from Rome?

8. What are Brutus' and Cassius' battle plans?

9. What reasons does Brutus give for his plan?

10. What does the ghost of Caesar tell Brutus?

Answers

1. It reaffirms Brutus' feelings that Cassius' friendship seems to be cooling down.

2. He doesn't want their troops to see them fighting.

3. Brutus disregarded letters Cassius wrote in defense of Lucius Pella, who was accused of taking bribes.

4. Brutus sent to Cassius for money to pay his soldiers and his request was denied.

5. Brutus says he is so honest that Cassius' threats mean nothing and pass him by like the idle wind.

6. He tells them to "Love and be friends as two such men should be." (Sc. 3, 150)

7. Between 70 and 100 senators, including Cicero, have been killed by Antony, Octavius, and Lepidus. Portia committed suicide by swallowing fire.

8. Brutus wants to march their armies from Sardis to Philippi and meet the enemy there. Cassius wants to remain where they are and have the enemy come to them.

9. He says the Sardians are not friendly. Their armies are at peak strength, and if they delay they will weaken. He says the opportunity to act is at hand, and if they do not take it, they will miss their chance for success.

10. The ghost says it is Brutus' evil spirit, and that it will see Brutus again at Philippi.

Suggested Essay Topics

1. Critics have said that Caesar has a stronger influence on the events, the outcome, and the characters in the play after his death than he did when he was living. Explain why you agree or disagree with this, and give reasons to support your opinions.

2. The critic G. Wilson Knight has described the importance of sleep in *Julius Caesar*. Sleep is mentioned by Brutus in his soliloquy in the first scene of Act II. It is brought up by Portia, and Calphurnia's dream is very significant. Discuss the sleep imagery in the play and show how it is important.

Act V

Act V, Scene 1

Summary

The setting is on the battlefield at Philippi. Antony and Octavius, at the head of their armies, are preparing to begin the battle. Through spies Antony knows the enemy is not ready for the fight. A messenger brings word that the battle is at hand. Before the combat, Antony and Octavius go into the field to exchange insults with Brutus and Cassius. They call each other traitors to Rome. Cassius says to Brutus that Antony would not be alive if Cassius had his way on the ides of March. They break off and plan to settle matters with their swords.

Cassius confides in Messala that he is reluctant to fight this battle on his birthday. He has seen signs that have convinced him that they are going to lose. But he is resigned to face whatever comes. Cassius and Brutus discuss what they will do if they are defeated. Both agree that they will not be led as captives back to Rome. Although Brutus is opposed to suicide, he will die before he is taken prisoner. They say their final good-byes and prepare for the battle.

Analysis

The battle to decide the fate of Rome is at hand. The growing conflict between Antony and young Octavius is foreshadowed by their exchange prior to the battle. Antony tries to tell Octavius to

fight on the left side of the field, but Octavius asserts himself and refuses to be ordered by Antony. When Antony asks him why he opposes him, Octavius responds, "I do not cross you, but I will do so." (21)

In the play the four generals never face one another in a decisive battle or even a fight. Instead, their confrontation is one of words, insults, and accusations, before the war begins. When Antony attacks Brutus and Cassius as villains and flatterers, Cassius takes the opportunity to tell Brutus, "I told you so." "Now, Brutus, thank yourself! / This tongue had not offended so today / If Cassius might have ruled." (49–51) His instincts about Antony are proven to be correct.

Superstition manifests itself again in this scene, as Cassius tells Messala that although he "held Epicurus strong" (did not believe in the supernatural influence on human affairs) he knows they are going to lose the battle because of the omens he has observed. The mighty eagles once perched on their battle ensigns, fed by his soldiers, have been replaced by ravens, crows and kites, scavengers that feast on corpses and "Fly o'er our heads and downward look on us / As we were sickly prey." (93–4)

The farewell between Brutus and Cassius is the last time Brutus will see his brother-in-law alive. Time is running out for both of them. Cassius speaks of the worst case scenario, and both agree that they will kill themselves rather than face defeat at the hands of Antony and Octavius. But win or lose, Brutus is content that whatever the outcome of the day's events, it will end what began on the ides of March.

Study Questions

1. What does Octavius report to Antony in the opening lines of the scene?

2. What is the cause of the disagreement between Antony and Octavius?

3. How does Antony insult Cassius and Brutus?

4. What is Cassius' response to Antony's insult?

5. Why is Cassius reluctant to fight the battle?

6. What are the omens he has observed?

7. Why would it be ironic if Cassius dies in the battle?

8. What is Brutus' attitude concerning suicide?

9. What is Brutus' response when Cassius asks if he is "contented to be led in triumph / Thorough the streets of Rome?" (119–20)

10. Why is Brutus anxious for the battle to begin?

Answers

1. The enemy is preparing to attack before Antony and Octavius are ready.

2. Antony tells Octavius to fight on the left side of the field, but Octavius says no.

3. He calls them villains and flatterers.

4. Cassius tells Brutus he should have listened to him and killed Antony when they killed Caesar.

5. From the signs and omens he is sure they will lose.

6. The eagles that were perched on their battle flags flew away and were replaced by ravens, crows, and kites, birds that feed on dead bodies.

7. It is his birthday.

8. He condemned his father-in-law, Cato, for killing himself rather than live under Caesar. He thinks it cowardly and vile to commit suicide in fear of what may happen in the future.

9. Brutus says he will never go back to Rome as a prisoner.

10. Win or lose, he wants to end the work that began on the ides of March.

Suggested Essay Topics

1. In literature the *climax* is defined as the highest point of action in a story, where the conflict is resolved. The battle between Cassius and Brutus and Antony and Octavius would seem to be the climax of the play, but this confrontation never takes place. When do you think the climax of the play occurs? Give reasons for your opinions.

2. Write a character sketch of Brutus, Cassius, Antony, Octavius and Caesar based on their actions, what they say, and what others say about them. What are their strong points and their weaknesses? Which character is the most interesting in your opinion and why?

Act V, Scenes 2 and 3

New Character:

Cato: *Brutus' brother-in-law and a soldier in his army*

Summary

The battle begins as Brutus orders Messala to send all of his

legions against Octavius' army. While Brutus gains the advantage
on another part of the field, Cassius is in retreat, surrounded by
Antony's forces. Pindarus, the slave of Cassius, enters with a warning for his master to fall back further. But Cassius decides that he
has retreated far enough. He asks his friend, Titinius, to ride his
horse and determine if the soldiers in his tents are friend or enemy. As Pindarus climbs the hill to report Titinius' progress, Cassius considers the real possibility that his life has reached its end
on his birthday. Pindarus describes Titinius overtaken and surrounded by horsemen, and as Titinius dismounts, he is captured
by the cheering soldiers.

  Cassius, ashamed that he has lived to see his best friend taken
by the enemy, promises to give Pindarus his freedom in exchange
for Pindarus ending Cassius' life by stabbing him.

  After Cassius' death Pindarus runs from the battlefield, and

Titinius, holding a wreath of flowers, returns with Messala and the news of Brutus' victory. They discover the body of Cassius and Messala leaves to tell Brutus the bad news. When Titinius is alone with Cassius' body, he places the wreath on Cassius' head and then he kills himself with Cassius' sword, as a final act of loyalty to his friend.

When Brutus enters with young Cato and Messala, they find two dead bodies to be mourned. Brutus says that the carnage is the spirit of Caesar, who is "mighty yet . . . and turns our swords / in our own proper entrails." (Sc. 3, 105–107)

Since the first fight was not decisive—Cassius was defeated by Antony, while Octavius was defeated by Brutus—preparations are made for the final battle.

Analysis

Throughout the play Brutus has been the noble hero, who has made errors only because of his honesty, moral principles, or political naivete. In this scene Cassius, perhaps the least noble of the main characters in he play, rises in stature. Here, however, he makes the one mistake that will prove fatal. His army is in retreat and on the verge of mutiny. They are surrounded by Antony, when Brutus' troops, gaining the advantage over Octavius, stop fighting to loot the dead bodies instead of supporting Cassius' army. When Pindarus, the slave Cassius captured years before in Parthia, announces, "Mark Antony is in your tents, my lord. / Fly therefore, noble Cassius, fly far off," (Sc. 3, 10–11) the "noble" Cassius is determined to make his stand and not retreat. When Cassius asks his friend Titinius to take his horse and ride down to see who is in his tents, Titinius indicates his love, honor, and respect for Cassius by his quick actions. He is ready and willing to put his own life on the line for his friend. "I will be here again even with a thought." (Sc. 3, 20)

Cassius' fatal error comes when he infers from Pindarus' account that Titinius was captured by enemy troops. It is another example of how subjective interpretation effects the actions of another. True to his word, Cassius makes good on his pledge to Brutus to commit suicide rather than surrender. He calls on Pindarus to return the kindness Cassius once showed him. When

Pindarus was captured in battle, Cassius spared his life, evoking a promise from him to do whatever Cassius asked of him. Now Cassius grants Pindarus his freedom in exchange for stabbing him when his head is turned. It is Pindarus' words that express his feelings. He would rather Cassius be alive and remain his slave. "So I am free, yet would not so have been, / Durst I have done my will. — O Cassius!—" (Sc. 3, 52–53)

The arrival of Titinius and Messala provides an explanation of the events misinterpreted by Cassius. The troops that surrounded Titinius were Brutus' men. Their shout was one of joy. The garland Titinius carries, to be presented to Cassius, is a token of Brutus' victory over Octavius.

Titinius shows his love for Cassius by his words and his actions. After sending Messala to bring the bad news to Brutus, Titinius kills himself with Cassius' sword. His final words are a tribute to his friend. "Brutus, come apace, / And see how I regarded Caius Cassius.— / By your leave, gods, this is a Roman's part. / Come Cassius' sword, and find Titinius' heart!" (Sc. 3, 97–100)

Brutus' reaction to their deaths is one of sorrow and tribute. He calls them "the last of all the Romans" (Sc. 3, 111) and says that Rome can never again produce such a breed. Although Cassius is not the tragic hero of the play, in death he has grown in stature.

The scene ends with Cassius' body being sent to Thasos, a Greek island in the Aegean, to await funeral rites, as Brutus readies his troops to "try fortune in a second fight." (Sc. 3, 123)

Study Questions

1. What order does Brutus give Messala in the battle?
2. How does Cassius try to prevent the retreat?
3. What news does Pindarus bring the retreating Cassius?
4. Why does Cassius ask Pindarus to describe Titinius' ride instead of doing so himself?
5. What does Pindarus describe?
6. What request does Cassius make of Pindarus?
7. What is ironic about the way Cassius dies?
8. What is the message Titinius has for Cassius?
9. How does Titinius show his high regard for Cassius?
10. Why does Brutus plan to send Cassius' body to Thasos for burial?

Answers

1. Brutus tells him to ride and order his army to attack Octavius' flank (wing).
2. He killed his own ensign (flag carrier) when the soldier retreated, causing Cassius' troops to follow the flag.

3.   Antony's troops are in Cassius' tents.

4.   He says that he has bad eyesight.

5.   Titinius is surrounded. He is taken and the soldiers shout for joy at his capture.

6.   He asks Pindarus to kill him in exchange for his freedom.

7.   He is killed on his birthday by the same sword that killed Caesar.

8.   Brutus has won his battle, and he brings a wreath of victory to present to Cassius.

9.   He kills himself with Cassius' sword.

10. He doesn't want his army to become depressed because of Cassius' death as they plan for the final battle.

Suggested Essay Topics

1.   Caesar considered Cassius a threat, a dangerous man who thought too much. Brutus called his brother-in-law "the last of all the Romans." Research the life of Cassius. Whose evaluation of Cassius is closer to the truth? Who is the real Cassius?

2.   Who do you think makes a better leader, a pragmatist (a practical, political person like Cassius) or an idealist (a man of principle such as Brutus)? Can a leader ever be both? Support your conclusions with specific references to the events of the play.

Act V, Scenes 4 and 5

New Characters:

Clitus, Dardanus, Strato, and Volumnius: *soldiers in Brutus' army*

Summary

At the height of the second battle Brutus charges into the field. Young Cato is killed and Lucilius, an officer in Brutus' army, is captured. To confuse the enemy soldiers, Lucilius tells them he is

Brutus, and offers them money to kill him. Antony identifies their captive and tells the soldiers to keep Lucilius safely under guard.

On another part of the field, after hours of fighting, Brutus and his men are in retreat. They have lost the war. Brutus begs Clitus, Volumnius, and Dardanus to assist him in his suicide, but they decline and run off as Antony and Octavius advance. Brutus convinces Strato to hold his sword while Brutus runs onto it and kills himself.

Octavius and Antony arrive with Lucilius and Messala under guard. When they ask for Brutus, Strato says his master is safe from capture and humiliation. Octavius offers amnesty for those who served Brutus and takes them into his army, restoring order after the chaos of civil war. Antony praises Brutus, calling him a noble

Roman and an honest man, the best of the conspirators. The play ends with Octavius making plans to bury the dead, including Brutus, who will be given an honorable soldier's burial, and spread the news of their great victory.

Analysis

The end arrives as Brutus sees his soldiers and his friends killed or captured. Lucilius is taken by Antony's soldiers. He tries to con-

fuse them by claiming that he is Brutus, to allow the real Brutus to escape. But Antony recognizes him and tells his soldiers, "Give him all kindness. I had rather have / Such men my friends than enemies." (Sc. 4, 29–30) Antony seems to be recruiting allies for a future clash with Octavius.

Brutus now realizes he has lost. "Our enemies have beat us to the pit. / It is more worthy to leap in ourselves / Than tarry till they push us." (Sc. 5, 27–29) Brutus is in tears when he pleads for someone to assist him in his plan to kill himself, but Clitus, Dardanus and Volumnius turn down his request as "not an office for a friend, my lord." (Sc. 5, 33)

Brutus says his final farewells, content that he is going to his death knowing that what he did was right for Rome. He is still unaware that he was tricked into the conspiracy by Cassius. He tells his "poor remains of friends" "My heart doth joy that yet in all my life / I found no man but he was true to me." (Sc. 5, 38–39) It is Strato who proves to be Brutus' best friend, agreeing to hold his sword while Brutus impales himself on the blade. His last words are addressed to Caesar's spirit. "Caesar, now be still. / I killed not thee with half so good a will." (Sc. 5, 56–57)

The arrival of Octavius and Antony gives the play closure and restores the world to its rightful order. By granting amnesty to the rebellious soldiers, Octavius ends the civil war that has torn Rome apart. A final peace is made with Brutus, the real tragic hero of the play. Antony honors Brutus and his reputation in death even though he attacked him in life before the battle. He calls him "the noblest Roman of them all." (Sc. 5, 74) He recognizes that all of the others acted out of envy for Caesar, but Brutus acted for the common good. Antony says of Brutus something he might have said of Caesar in his funeral oration: "His life was gentle and the elements / So mixed in him that nature might stand up / And say to all the world 'This was a man!'" (Sc. 5, 79–81)

With the final words from Octavius—the new Caesar—the Roman world is settled, at least for now, as the play ends.

Study Questions

1. What happens to young Cato?

2. How does Lucilius try to confuse the enemy troops?

3. What does Lucilius request of the two soldiers?

4. What does Antony do when he recognizes Lucilius?

5. Why does Brutus say he wants to commit suicide?

6. What is the one thing Brutus says he is happy about before he dies?

7. How does Brutus die?

8. How does Strato answer Messala's inquiry about Brutus?

9. How does Octavius restore order to Rome after the battle?

10. How does Antony regard Brutus at the end of the play?

Answers

1. He is killed in the battle.

2. Lucilius tells his capturers that he is Brutus.

3. He offers them money and asks them to kill him.

4. He tells his men to treat Lucilius well and keep him safe because he wants him as a friend.

5. He uses the metaphor of a pit. His enemies have forced them to the edge and it is more noble to jump in than be pushed in.

6. Brutus is happy that in all his life his friends have been truthful and honest with him. The irony is that he was tricked by Cassius into joining the conspiracy against Caesar.

7. Strato holds his sword and Brutus runs onto it, stabbing himself.

8. He tells him that Brutus is safe from bondage (captivity), and that he was not conquered by his enemy. Brutus only conquered himself.

9. He gives amnesty to those who fought on the side of Brutus, and he invites them into his army.

10. He calls him a noble Roman who did what he thought was

right. He was the only one who acted against Caesar for unselfish reasons, the common good.

Suggested Essay Topics

1. Some critics contend the play should have been titled *Marcus Brutus* instead of *Julius Caesar* because he is the real tragic hero of the play. Discuss this idea in a short essay and give your reasons why you agree or disagree.

2. Caesar and Brutus had a great deal in common. Both men were misled and manipulated by their friends. Show how this is true in terms of what happens to each of them in the course of the play.

3. According to some critics, *Julius Caesar* is misinterpreted by modern audiences who are concerned with democracy and freedom. According to these critics, Shakespeare had a different view of things. He lived under a monarch in a time of peace and prosperity, after a series of bloody civil wars. To Shakespeare, Brutus was a villain in this play and not a hero. He murdered a popular ruler and destroyed the social order. Do you agree or disagree with this interpretation of the play? Provide evidence from the play to support your opinions.

Sample Analytical Paper Topics

The following paper topics are based on the entire play. Following each topic is a thesis and sample outline. Use these as a starting point for your paper.

Topic #1

"Power tends to corrupt and absolute power corrupts absolutely." This statement by Lord Acton, sent in a letter to Bishop Mandell Creighton on April 5, 1887, provides the basis for understanding the effects of power on the heads of state, and it furnishes an insight into one of the main themes in the play *Julius Caesar*.

Write a paper that shows how power affects the characters, the events, and the outcome of the play.

Outline

I.   Thesis Statement: Julius Caesar *is a play that illustrates the theme expressed by Lord Acton that power corrupts and absolute power corrupts absolutely. This can be illustrated by studying the actions of the main characters in the play.*

II. Background

    A. Caesar, Pompey, and Crassus rule Rome (triumvirate)

    B. Power struggle between Pompey and Caesar

    C. Civil war ends with the death of Pompey

    D. Caesar's rise to power

III. Concern for the Republic and Caesar's growing power

    A. Flavius and Marullus disperse the crowd to minimize Caesar's power base and protect the Roman Republic

    B. A view of Caesar's power on the feast of Lupercal, how he deals with Calphurnia and Antony

IV. The Conspiracy against Caesar

    A. Cassius and Brutus discuss what must be done to prevent Caesar from destroying Rome

        1. Cassius—wants personal power

        2. Brutus—wants the good of Rome

        3. Cassius exploits his power over Brutus by forging letters that will sway him

    B. Brutus joins the plot to prevent Caesar's abuse of power and Brutus assumes the leadership, imposing his wishes on the others

    C. The conspirators have the power of life and death in Rome and they decide who will live and who will die

V. The Assassination

    A. Caesar's death causes a power struggle in Rome as the conspirators become the new leaders

    B. Brutus' funeral speech and his rise to power as the crowds want to make him king

    C. Antony's funeral speech and his rise to power unleashing the mob on Rome for his personal reasons

VI. The Aftermath in Rome

    A. Antony, Octavius, and Lepidus are changed by their new-found power

    1.   They make a death list to consolidate their power in Rome

    2.   They change Caesar's will and his generous legacy to Rome

    3.   Antony's abuse of Lepidus for his political ends

  B.   The growing conflict between Antony and Octavius

VII. The Aftermath in Greece

  A.   The conflict between Brutus and Cassius

  B.   The impending war

VIII. The Civil War

  A.   The deaths of Brutus and Cassius

  B.   Antony and Octavius rise to power

Topic #2

Any analysis of *Julius Caesar* would not be complete without considering the matter of subjective interpretation. Throughout the play characters and events are judged not by what is actually happening, but by one or more characters' interpretation of these things.

Write a paper that examines these subjective interpretations of characters and events throughout the play, providing examples to support your conclusions.

Outline

I.   Thesis Statement: *Understanding* Julius Caesar *depends on realizing that the audience's attitude toward the characters, and the events of the play, are not rooted in reality, but in a subjective interpretation of reality.*

II.   Act I

  A.   Flavius and Marullus paint a biased and negative picture of Caesar based on their support of Pompey

    1.   What did Pompey do that was so good?

    2.   What did Caesar do that was so bad?

B. Caesar is revealed in his exchanges with Antony, Calphurnia, and the soothsayer

C. Cassius describes Caesar to Brutus as physically weak and unfit to rule Rome

1. Cassius saved Caesar's life while swimming

2. Caesar cried like a sick girl in Spain

D. Caesar's assessment of Cassius as a dangerous man is the opposite of Antony's opinion that Cassius is "a noble Roman, and well given." (Act I, Sc. 2, 197)

E. Caesar's behavior off stage is not seen by the audience but by Casca's biased account of events at the Coliseum

F. Cassius describes Caesar to Casca as a monster, whose abuse of power is shown by the gods sending supernatural omens and storms to warn Rome

III. Act II

A. Brutus bases his decision to kill Caesar not on what he has done, but on what he might do

1. Cassius has been influencing him for a month

2. Brutus has received many anonymous letters opposing the tyrant Caesar

B. The conspirators assessment of Antony is also subjective

1. To Cassius he is a danger to be eliminated

2. To Brutus he is only a "limb of Caesar" (Act II, Sc. 1, 165)

C. The interpretation of supernatural events

1. Calphurnia's dream is a sign that Caesar will be killed

2. Caesar sees it as a warning from the gods that he is a coward if he stays at home

3. Decius interprets it as Caesar being the strength, power, and lifeblood of Rome and it is his view that influences Caesar

IV. Act III

    A. Caesar's opinion of himself as "constant as the Northern Star," (Act III, Sc. 1, 66) incapable of changing his mind or making mistakes, although he has made several mistakes in judgment to this point

    B. To Cinna and Cassius the death of Caesar is a source of "Liberty, freedom and enfranchisement" (Act III, Sc.1, 81)

    C. To Antony, his death is the "ruins of the noblest man / That ever lived in the tide of times." (Act III, Sc. 1, 296–257) and the first step on the path to anarchy and bloody civil war

    D. Brutus' funeral speech attempts to cast Caesar an ambitious tyrant who would have destroyed the Republic and made slaves of everyone

    E. Antony's funeral speech shows a compassionate Caesar, who cried for suffering Romans, and a generous man who left money and land in his will for every citizen

    F. Antony's account of the murder of Caesar, although he did not witness it, stirs the angry mob to want revenge

V. Act IV

    A. Antony's assessment of Lepidus as being unfit to rule Rome

    B. Octavius' opinion that he is a "tried and valiant soldier" (Act IV, Sc. 1, 29)

    C. Cassius' reasons for not going to Philippi

    D. Brutus' opinions that the must go or lose the opportunity for success

VI. Act V

    A. In the parley before the battle both sides see themselves as true Romans and the others as the traitors

    B. Pindarus gives his subjective account of Titinius being captured by the enemy, and it results in Cassius' death

    C.   Antony's opinion of Brutus as "the noblest Roman of them all" (Act V, Sc. 5, 69) is in sharp contrast with his earlier view of Brutus as a murderer and flatterer

Topic #3

Superstition, in the opinion of Polybius, a Greek writer, was an important force in Rome and it plays a major part in *Julius Caesar*. Many decisions in the daily lives of the Romans were referred to the augurers, who could determine the will of the gods through ritual and sacrifice. Augurers decided the Roman calendar, and what days, were and were not suitable for conducting business. Caesar himself was an augurer, a position of influence in Roman society.

Write a paper that examines Roman superstition, and show the effects it had on the events and the outcome of the play.

Outline

I.   Thesis Statement: *Superstition is an important factor in determining the events and the outcome of* Julius Caesar, *a significant force throughout the course of the entire play.*

II.   The Feast of Lupercal

    A.   The play begins on a festival in honor of the god Pan, the god of fertility

    B.   Caesar indicates his superstition by directing Antony to touch Calphurnia during the race, to make her fertile and enable her to provide Caesar with an heir

    C.   The soothsayer provides a look into the future and a warning for Caesar

III. The Omens of Nature

    A.   Casca's account to Cicero of the unnatural events he has witnessed, which he interprets as the gods in a state of civil war, or intent on destroying the world

    B.   Cassius's account of the message from the gods, warning Rome of Caesar's growing power and the threat he poses for the Republic

IV. The Sacrifice of the Augurers

   A. Finding no heart in the beast is a warning to Caesar to remain home

   B. To Caesar it is a rebuke from the gods that he is a coward if he does not go out

V. Calphurnia's Dream—Caesar's statue spouting blood

   A. Calphurnia's interpretation it is a warning of Caesar's impending death

   B. Decius' favorable interpretation of the dream as a sign of Caesar's stature in Rome and the respect all the Romans have for him

VI. Signs before the Battle

   A. Caesar's ghost, an omen of Brutus' death

   B. The eagles on the ensign replaced by ravens and kites, a sign that Cassius and Brutus will lose the battle and die

SECTION EIGHT

Bibliography

Quotations are taken from the following edition:

Shakespeare, William. *The Tragedy of Julius Caesar.* New York: Washington Square Press/Folger Shakespeare Library, 1992.

Introducing...

MAXnotes

REA's Literature Study Guide

MAXnotes™ offer a fresh look at masterpieces of literature, presented in a liv and interesting fashion. **MAXnotes**™ offer the essentials of what you should kr about the work, including outlines, explanations and discussions of the p character lists, analyses, and historical context. **MAXnotes**™ are designed to h you think independently about literary works by raising various issues and thoug provoking ideas and questions. Written by literary experts who currently teach subject, **MAXnotes**™ enhance your understanding and enjoyment of the work

Available **MAXnotes**™ include the following:

Animal Farm	Huckleberry Finn	Of Mice and Men
Beowulf	I Know Why the	The Odyssey
The Canterbury Tales	Caged Bird Sings	Paradise Lost
Death of a Salesman	The Iliad	Plato's Republic
Divine Comedy I-Inferno	Julius Caesar	A Raisin in the Sun
Gone with the Wind	King Lear	Romeo and Juliet
The Grapes of Wrath	Les Misérables	The Scarlet Letter
Great Expectations	Macbeth	A Tale of Two Cities
The Great Gatsby	Moby Dick	To Kill a Mockingbird
Hamlet	1984	

RESEARCH & EDUCATION ASSOCIATION
61 Ethel Road W. • Piscataway, New Jersey 08854
Phone: (908) 819-8880

Please send me more information about MAXnotes™.

Name _____

Address _____

City _____ State _____ Zip _____

Available at your local bookstore or order directly from us by sending in coupon below.

REA's Test Prep
The Best in Test Preparatio

The REA "Test Preps" are far more comprehensive than any other test series. They contain more
with much more extensive explanations than others on the market. Each book provides sev
complete practice exams, based on the most recent tests given in the particular field. Every typ
question likely to be given on the exams is included. Each individual test is followed by a comp
answer key. **The answers are accompanied by full and detailed explanations.** By studying each
and the explanations which follow, students will become well-prepared for the actual exam.

REA has published over 40 Test Preparation volumes in several series. They include:

**Advanced Placement Exams
(APs)**
Biology
Calculus AB & Calculus BC
Chemistry
Computer Science
English Language & Composition
English Literature & Composition
European History
Government & Politics
Physics
Psychology
United States History

SAT II: Subject Tests
American History
Biology
Chemistry
French
German
Literature
Mathematics Level I, IIC
Physics
Spanish
Writing

Graduate Record Exams (GREs)
Biology
Chemistry
Computer Science
Economics
Engineering
General
History
Literature in English
Mathematics
Physics
Political Science
Psychology

ASVAB - Armed Service Vocational
Aptitude Battery

CBEST - California Basic Educational
Skills Test

CDL - Commercial Driver's License Exam

CLAST - College Level Academic Skills
Test

ELM - Entry Level Mathematics

ExCET - Exam for Certificatior
Educators in Texas

FE (EIT) - Fundamentals of
Engineering Exam

GED - High School Equivalenc
Diploma Exam (US & Canad
editions)

GMAT - Graduate Managemen
Admission Test

LSAT - Law School Admission

MCAT - Medical College Admi.
Test

NTE - National Teachers Exam

PSAT - Preliminary Scholastic
Assessment Test

SAT I - Reasoning Test

SAT I - Quick Study & Review

TASP - Texas Academic Skills
Program

TOEFL - Test of English as a
Foreign Language

RESEARCH & EDUCATION ASSOCIATION
61 Ethel Road W. • Piscataway, New Jersey 08854
Phone: (908) 819-8880

Please send me more information about your Test Prep Books

Name _____

Address _____

City _____ State _____ Zip _____